Beginning Robotics with Raspberry Pi and Arduino

Using Python and OpenCV

Jeff Cicolani

Beginning Robotics with Raspberry Pi and Arduino:

Using Python and OpenCV

Jeff Cicolani
Pflugerville, Texas, USA

ISBN-13 (pbk): 978-1-4842-3461-7   ISBN-13 (electronic): 978-1-4842-3462-4
https://doi.org/10.1007/978-1-4842-3462-4

Library of Congress Control Number: 2018937971

Managing Director, Apress Media LLC: Welmoed Spahr
Acquisitions Editor: Aaron Black
Development Editor: James Markham
Coordinating Editor: Jessica Vakili

Cover designed by eStudioCalamar

Cover image designed by Freepik (www.freepik.com)

Distributed to the book trade worldwide by Springer Science+Business Media New York, 233 Spring Street, 6th Floor, New York, NY 10013. Phone 1-800-SPRINGER, fax (201) 348-4505, e-mail orders-ny@springer-sbm.com, or visit www.springeronline.com. Apress Media, LLC is a California LLC and the sole member (owner) is Springer Science + Business Media Finance Inc (SSBM Finance Inc). SSBM Finance Inc is a **Delaware** corporation.

For information on translations, please e-mail rights@apress.com, or visit http://www.apress.com/rights-permissions.

Apress titles may be purchased in bulk for academic, corporate, or promotional use. eBook versions and licenses are also available for most titles. For more information, reference our Print and eBook Bulk Sales web page at http://www.apress.com/bulk-sales.

Any source code or other supplementary material referenced by the author in this book is available to readers on GitHub via the book's product page, located at www.apress.com/978-1-4842-3461-7. For more detailed information, please visit http://www.apress.com/source-code.

Printed on acid-free paper

For Martha, my beautiful and patient wife, for putting up with random robot parts strewn about the house, pretty much constantly

Table of Contents

About the Author

 **Jeff Cicolani** currently lives in the Austin, Texas, area with his wife, two dogs, and dozen or so robots. He is currently working as an embedded systems engineer, building robotic and automated platforms for an AI (artificial intelligence) company in Austin. His journey to robotics was circuitous, taking him through an odd career path that included systems analysis and design and database programming. In 2012, he joined The Robot Group in Austin, where he joined a group of robotics enthusiasts and began building robots as a hobby. In 2016, he became president of The Robot Group. In this role, he leads the group in their mission to promote STEM (science, technology, engineering, and mathematics) education through robotics. He is currently working to develop a better understanding of advanced robotics through ROS (the robot operating system) and machine learning.

About the Technical Reviewer

Massimo Nardone has more than 22 years of experiences in security, web/mobile development, cloud, and IT architecture. His true IT passions are security and Android.

He has been programming and teaching how to program with Android, Perl, PHP, Java, VB, Python, C/C++, and MySQL for more than 20 years.

He holds a Master of Science degree in Computing Science from the University of Salerno, Italy.

He has worked as a project manager, software engineer, research engineer, chief security architect, information security manager, PCI/SCADA auditor, and senior lead IT security/cloud/SCADA architect for many years.

His technical skills include security, Android, cloud, Java, MySQL, Drupal, Cobol, Perl, web and mobile development, MongoDB, D3, Joomla, Couchbase, C/C++, WebGL, Python, Pro Rails, Django CMS, Jekyll, Scratch, and more.

He currently works as a chief information security officer (CISO) for Cargotec Oyj. He worked as visiting lecturer and supervisor for exercises at the Networking Laboratory of the Helsinki University of Technology (Aalto University). He holds four international patents (PKI, SIP, SAML, and Proxy areas).

Introduction

Robotics does not have to be difficult. In this book, I introduce you to the field of robotics. The journey will be challenging; it's intended to be. But by the end of the book, you will have hands-on exposure to many of the fundamental—and not so fundamental—aspects of robotics. You will work with hardware, assemble and solder a circuit board, write code in two programming languages, install and configure a Linux environment, and work with computer vision. Everything else you do with robots will be an extension of the lessons learned in this book.

Who This book Is For

This book is for those who are new to electronics and IoT; those who have never used a Raspberry Pi or Arduino separately, let alone together.

This book is for the hobbyist who is interested in learning a little more about working with robots. Perhaps you've built a few circuits with an Arduino or a custom home entertainment system with a Raspberry Pi, and now you are curious about what goes into building a robot. You will learn how these two devices work together to provide very powerful capabilities.

This book is for the entrepreneur who needs to learn more about technology; someone who doesn't necessarily have the time to read through many different books on Arduino, Raspberry Pi, electronics, or programming; someone who is looking for a broad yet condensed introduction to some of the fundamentals.

This book is also for the student who wants to take their robot-building experience beyond bricks and puzzle-piece programming; someone who wants to work with hardware and software that more closely resembles what they might see in college or in the professional world.

No assumptions are made about experience or background in technology. As you go through the chapters, you may find parts that you are already familiar with, and you can skip ahead. But if you are new to these topics, I try to provide you with a quick but easy introduction.

Chapter Overview

You start by learning about the Raspberry Pi and how to work with it. You download and install the Raspbian operating system, and then configure the Pi for our project. The goal is to set up your system to be able to easily access your robot and write your code directly on it.

Once you are able to access your Pi remotely, in Chapter 3, you delve into programming with Python. I'll show you how to write simple programs on the Raspberry Pi. I also take you beyond the basics and cover some intermediate topics, such as modules and classes. This is one of the longest chapters since there is a lot of material to cover.

From there, you learn how to interface the Raspberry Pi with external electronics, such as sensors and LEDs, through the Pi's GPIO header. Chapter 4 discusses the different ways of addressing the pins on the header, some of the functionality exposed through the header, and how to use an ultrasonic rangefinder to detect objects. This gets you ready for the next chapter, which introduces the Arduino.

In Chapter 5, you connect the Arduino to the Raspberry Pi. I discuss some of the reasons you want to do this. I show you how to work with the Arduino IDE to write programs. I cover serial communication between the two boards and how to pass information back and forth between them. We do this using the same ultrasonic rangefinder used in the previous chapter.

Chapter 6 has you turning motors with your Raspberry Pi. You use a special board called a *hat*, or *plate*, to control the motors. This is where I introduce another skill that you will inevitably need in robotics: soldering.

The header and terminals need to be soldered on to the board that was selected for this purpose. The nice thing about soldering headers and terminal blocks is that it's hard to damage anything, and you will get plenty of practice.

Chapter 7 is where we bring it all together. You build the robot, and I discuss some of the physical characteristics of robotics. I cover some of the design considerations that you will need to keep in mind when you design your own chassis. Although I am listing a specific chassis kit for this project, you do not need to use the same one. In fact, I encourage you to explore other options to find the one that is right for you.

In Chapter 8, I introduce another type of sensor—the IR sensor, and I show you how to use a very common control algorithm called a PID controller. I talk about the various types of IR sensors and where you want to use them. (The chapter on PID control discusses what it is and why you want to use it.)

Chapter 9 is about computer vision, where you see the true power of the Raspberry Pi. In this chapter, I cover an open source package called OpenCV. By the end of Chapter 9, your little robot will be chasing a ball around the table.

I leave you with some parting thoughts in Chapter 10. I provide a few tips that I picked up, and I give you a glimpse into my workflow and tools. After that, you will be ready to begin your own adventures in robotics.

CHAPTER 1

Introduction to Robotics

The word *robotics* can mean a lot of things. For some people, it is anything that moves by itself; kinetic art is robotics. To other people, robotics means something that is mobile or something that can move itself from place to place. There is actually a field called mobile robotics; automatic vacuum cleaners, such as a Roomba or a Neato, fall into this category. To me robotics falls somewhere in between kinetic art and mobile robotics.

A *robot* is technology that applies logic to perform a task in an automated manner. This is a fairly broad definition, but robotics is a fairly broad field. It can cover everything from a child's toy to the automatic parallel parking capabilities in some automobiles. We build a small mobile robot in this book.

Many of the principals that you are exposed to in this book are easily transferable to other areas. In fact, we will go through the entire process of building a robot from beginning to end. A little later in this chapter, I go over the project that we will build. At that time, I will provide a list of the parts used in in this book. These parts include sensors, drivers, motors, and so forth. You are welcome to use whatever you have on hand because, for the most part, everything we go through in this book can be applied to other projects.

© Jeff Cicolani 2018
J. Cicolani, *Beginning Robotics with Raspberry Pi and Arduino*,
https://doi.org/10.1007/978-1-4842-3462-4_1

Robotics Basics

I like to tell people who are new to robotics, or are just robotics curious, is that a robot consists of three elements.

- The ability to gather data
- The ability to process, or do something with the gathered data
- The ability to interact with the environment

In the following chapters, we apply this principal to build a small mobile robot. We will use ultrasonic rangefinders and infrared sensors to gather data about the environment. Specifically, we will identify when there is an object to be avoided, when we are about to drive off the edge of a table, and the contrast between the table and the line that we will follow. Once we have this data, we will apply logic to determine the appropriate response.

We will use Python in a Linux environment to process the information and send commands to our motors. I chose Python as the programming language because it is easy to learn, and you don't have to have a complex development environment to build some pretty complex applications.

Our interaction with the environment will be simply to control the speed and direction of motors. This will allow our robot to move about freely on the table or floor. There really isn't much to driving a motor. We will look at two ways of doing it: with a motor driver made for the Raspberry Pi and with a common motor controller.

This book is intended to be challenging. I cover some pretty complex material and I do it quickly. There is no way that I can provide detailed coverage on any of these topics, but I hope to get you to a functional robot by the end of the book. In each chapter, I try to provide you with more resources to follow up on the topics discussed. You will struggle at times; I did and I frequently still do.

Not everyone will be interested in all the subjects. The expectation is that you will expand on the areas that interest you the most outside of this book. Persistence pays off.

At the end of the book, I add a little more challenge. In Chapter 9, we begin leveraging the real power of the Raspberry Pi. We look at computer vision. Specifically, we look at an open source package called OpenCV (CV stands for *computer vision*). It is a common and very powerful collection of utilities that make working with images and video streams very easy. It's also a six-hour build on the most recent version of the Raspberry Pi. To make things a little easier and a lot less time-consuming, I have available for download a version of the operating system with OpenCV already installed. I discuss this more in Chapter 2.

Linux and Robotics

Linux is a Unix-based operating system. It is very popular with programmers and computer scientists because it's simple and straightforward. They seem to enjoy the text-based interface of the terminal. Yet, for many others, including me, Linux can be very challenging. So, why in the world would I choose this environment for an introduction-to-robotics book? The answer to that question is threefold.

First, when you work with robotics, you eventually have to confront Linux. That's just a fact. You can do a lot without ever typing a single sudo command, but you will have limited capabilities. The sudo command stands for *super user do* in Linux. This tells the operating system that you are about to perform a protected function that requires more than general user access. You will learn more about this when we begin working with the Raspberry Pi.

Second, Linux is challenging. As I stated before, this book will challenge you. If you have worked in Linux before, then this reason doesn't apply to you. However, if you are new to Linux, the Raspberry Pi, or working in a command line, then some of the things that we do will be challenging. And that's good. You're learning something new and it should be a challenge.

Third, and this is by far the most important, the Raspberry Pi uses Linux. Yes, you can install other operating systems on the Pi, but it was designed and intended to use Linux. In fact, the Raspberry Pi has its own flavor of Linux called Raspbian. This is the recommended operating system, so it is what we'll use. One of the nice things about using a prebuilt operating system, besides its ease of use, is many of the tools are already installed and ready to go.

Since we are using Linux, we will use command-line instructions extensively. This is where most new users have problems. Command-line code is entered via a terminal. Raspbian has a Windows-style interface that we will use, but much of it uses the terminal. A terminal window is available in the graphical user interface (GUI), so we will use that. However, when we set up the Pi, we will set it up to boot into terminal mode by default. Getting to the GUI is only a simple `startx` command. All of this is covered in Chapter 2.

Sensors and GPIO

GPIO stands for *general-purpose input/output*. It represents all the various connections to devices. The Raspberry Pi has a lot of GPIO options: HDMI, USB, audio, and so forth. However, when I talk about GPIO in this book, I'm generally referring to the 40-pin GPIO header. This header provides direct access to most of the board's functionality. I discuss this in Chapter 2.

Arduino also has GPIO. In fact, one could argue that Arduino is all GPIO and nothing else. This isn't far from the truth given that all the other connections are there to allow you to communicate with and power the AVR chip at the heart of the Arduino.

All of these headers and GPIO connections are there so we can access sensors outside the boards themselves. A *sensor* is a device that gathers data. There are many different types of sensors, and all serve a purpose. Sensors can be used for detecting light levels, the range to an object, temperature, speed, and so forth. In particular, we will use GPIO headers with an ultrasonic rangefinder and an IR detector.

Motion and Control

One thing that most definitions of a robot have in common is that it needs to be able to move. Sure, you can have a robot that doesn't actually move, but this type of device generally falls under the moniker of *IoT*, the Internet of Things.

There are many ways to add motion to your project. The most common is the use of motors. But you can also use solenoids, air, or water pressure. I discuss motors more in Chapter 6.

Although it is possible to drive a motor directly off a Raspberry Pi or an Arduino board, it is strongly discouraged. Motors tend to draw more current than the processors on the boards can handle. Instead, it is recommended that you use a motor controller. Like motors, motor controllers come in many forms. The motor control board that we will use is accessed through the Raspberry Pi's header. I also discuss how to drive motors with an L298N dual motor controller.

Raspberry Pi and Arduino

We will use a Raspberry Pi (see Figure 1-1) in conjunction with an Arduino (see Figure 1-2) as our robot's processing platform.

Figure 1-1. *Raspberry Pi 3 B+*

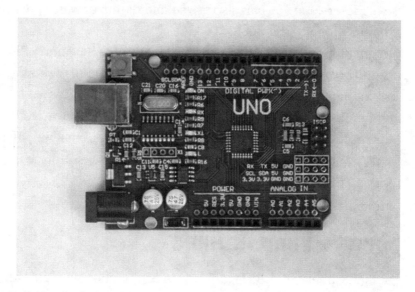

Figure 1-2. *Arduino Uno*

The Raspberry Pi is a single board computer that is about the size of a credit card. Despite its small size, it is a very capable device. The Pi runs a version of Linux that was customized to work on the ARM processor that drives it. This puts a lot of functionality into a small device that is easy to embed into things like robots. But, although it is a great computer, there are a few places where it does not excel. One area is interfacing with external devices. It can work with sensors and external devices, but the Arduino does this much better.

Arduino is another small processing device that is readily available and easy to use. Unlike a Raspberry Pi, however, it does not have the capacity for a full operating system. Rather than running a microprocessor like the ARM, it uses a different type of chip called a *microcontroller*. The difference is that a microcontroller is specifically designed to interact with sensors, motors, lights, and all kinds of devices. It directly interacts with these external devices. The Pi works through many layers of processing before it ever reaches the pins that a device is connected to.

By combining the Raspberry Pi and the Arduino, we are able to leverage what each does best. The Raspberry Pi offers the high-level processing power of a full computer. Arduino provides the raw control over external devices. The Pi allows us to process a video stream from a simple USB camera; whereas the Arduino allows us to gather the information from the various sensors, and apply logic to make sense of all that data, and then return concise findings to the Pi.

You will learn more about the Raspberry Pi in Chapter 2. Later on, you will connect an Arduino to the Pi and learn about programming it, as well as how to pass information back and forth between the Arduino and the Pi.

Project Overview

In this book, we will build a small mobile robot. The robot is designed to demonstrate the lessons that you learn in each chapter. However, before we can actually build the robot, we need to cover a lot of material and lay the foundation for future lessons.

The Robot

The robot that we will build is a small two- or four-wheeled autonomous rover. It will be able to detect obstacles and the edge of a table, and to follow a line. The chassis that I selected is a four-wheeled robot, but there are other designs suitable for this project (see Figures 1-3 and 1-4).

Figure 1-3.   *The front of our robot shows the ultrasonic sensors and Pi T Cobbler on a breadboard*

Figure 1-4. *The back of our robot shows the Raspberry Pi and motor control board*

Although I provide a list of the parts that I used for the project, you are welcome to use whatever parts you wish. The important thing is that they behave in a similar manner as those I have listed.

Bill of Materials (BOM)

For the most part, I tried to keep the list of materials as generic as possible. There are a couple of items that are vendor specific. I chose them because they provide a lot of functionality and convenience. The DC & Stepper motor controller and the Pi T-Cobbler are from an online retailer called Adafruit, which is a great resource for parts, tutorials, and inspiration. The chassis kit is from an online retailer called ServoCity, which produces many mechanical parts for robotics.

The following are the specialty parts (shown in Figure 1-5) that we use in this book:

- Runt Rover Junior robot chassis from ServoCity.com

- Adafruit DC & Stepper Motor HAT for Raspberry Pi – Mini Kit PID: 2348

- GPIO Stacking Header for Pi A+/B+/Pi 2/Pi 3 – Extra-long 2×20 Pins PID: 2223 (allows the use of additional plates and the Cobbler to attach to the breadboard)

- Assembled Pi T-Cobbler Plus – GPIO Breakout – Pi A+, B+, Pi 2, Pi 3, Zero PID: 2028

Figure 1-5. *Runt Rover chassis parts and the Pi T Cobbler, ribbon cable, motor control hat, and extended header*

The following parts (shown in Figure 1-6) are fairly generic and can be purchased from most vendors:

- Raspberry Pi 3 – Model B – ARMv8 with 1G RAM

- Arduino Uno

- 4 × AA battery holder with on/off switch (powers the motors)

- USB Battery Pack – 2200 mAh Capacity – 5V 1A Output PID: 1959 (powers the Raspberry Pi)

- Half-size breadboard

- Ultrasonic sensors – HC-SR04

  You may want to get a few of these. As you will discover, ultrasonic sensors are unreliable at angles, and it is good to have an array of them. I use at least three on most of my projects.

- A collection of jumper wires (see Figure 1-7)

  You need both male-to-male jumpers and male-to-female jumpers. It is a good idea to get them in a number of colors. Black and red are used for powering your devices. A collection of other colors helps you make sense of your circuits. Fortunately, you can get jumpers of all types made out of a multicolored ribbon cable.

- USB cables for your Arduino

- A micro USB cable for your Raspberry Pi

- A common USB phone charger, preferably one for a modern smartphone or tablet that can provide 2 amps of power

- An HDMI TV or computer monitor

  Most computer monitors do not have HDMI ports on them. You can get HDMI-to-DVI converters that allow you to use your existing monitor, however.

- A USB keyboard and mouse (I like the Logitech K400 wireless keyboard and touchpad combination, but there are countless options out there)

- A network-connected computer

- Wi-Fi or Ethernet cable for the Pi

Figure 1-6. *Common parts: Raspberry Pi, Arduino Uno, ultrasonic sensor, battery holder, and breadboard*

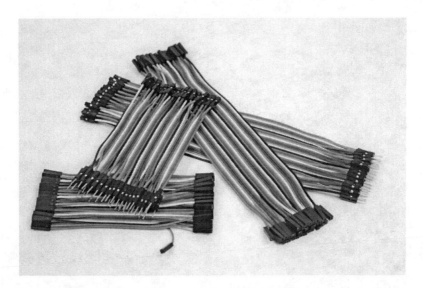

Figure 1-7. *Jumpers in ribbon cable form. Pull off what you need*

You don't need to get fancy with the monitor and keyboard. Once you read Chapter 2, where we install and configure the Raspberry Pi , you no longer need them. I have a couple of the wireless keyboards because I usually have several projects going at once. For a monitor, I simply use one of my computer monitors with an HDMI-to-DVI adapter.

If you are not using a chassis kit with motors and wheels included, you also need the following parts (see Figure 1-8):

- Hobby gearmotor – 200 RPM (pair)

- Wheel – 65mm (rubber tire, pair)

Figure 1-8. *DC geared motor and wheels*

If you do not want to use the Adafruit Motor and Stepper Hat, you can also use virtually any motor controller, although each one has a different interface and code. A common and fairly popular option is the L298N Dual Motor Controller (see Figure 1-9).

Figure 1-9. *The L298N dual motor controller module comes in numerous varieties, but essentially work the same*

There are a few other supplies that I keep around because they are used in virtually every project . In Chapter 7, we assemble the robot; you'll need also double-sided foam mounting tape, 4-inch zip ties, and self-adhesive Velcro. As you continue in robotics, you'll find yourself turning to these items a lot. In fact, you may want to stock up on various sizes of zip ties. Trust me.

Summary

Getting started in robotics does not need to be difficult. It is challenging, however. This book is an introduction to a few of the skills that you need to develop if you are to succeed in this field. The robot that we build introduces you to the Raspberry Pi, Linux, Arduino, sensors, and computer vision. These skills easily scale into larger robot and other similar projects.

CHAPTER 2

An Introduction to Raspberry Pi

The purpose of this book is to challenge you to build a simple robot that will be expanded over time. This book is intended to be difficult; however, it isn't too difficult or unnecessarily complicated. You'll experience plenty of complications along the way, but the installation of the operating system on your Raspberry Pi does not need to be one of them.

Downloading and Installing Raspbian

There are, essentially, two methods of installing the operating system (OS) on your Pi.

The first involves downloading the latest Raspbian image, writing it to an SD card, and going from there. This method requires the installation of a third-party software package that writes a bootable image on an SD card. The advantage is that it takes less room on your SD card. If you're using a minimum 8GB SD card, this may be helpful; if you went bigger, then this consideration is moot.

Whereas the direct installation is not all that complicated (rather easy actually), there's an easier way that doesn't involve installing additional software on your system. NOOBS (New Out Of the Box Software) is designed to make the installation and configuration of your Raspberry Pi

© Jeff Cicolani 2018
J. Cicolani, *Beginning Robotics with Raspberry Pi and Arduino*,
https://doi.org/10.1007/978-1-4842-3462-4_2

easier. It allows you to select from multiple operating systems and simply install. However, the NOOBS package remains on the SD card and eats up valuable space. It does allow you to go back and repair your OS or change the OS completely, but that can be handled manually quite easily.

In the end, the choice is yours. I'll go over both options so that you can choose whichever installation path works best for you. No matter which option you choose, your journey begins at the Raspbian download page at www.raspberrypi.org/downloads/ (see Figure 2-1).

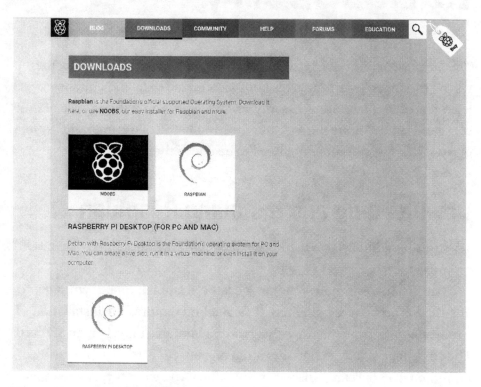

Figure 2-1. *Raspbian download screen*

Raspbian with OpenCV

Toward the end of this book, we will work with computer vision to show you why you should use a Raspberry Pi rather than a less capable platform. In order to do that, however, you need to install OpenCV on your Pi. Unfortunately, there is no simple OpenCV installer for the Raspberry Pi. Because the Pi runs on an ARM processor, the package has to be compiled from source code, which is a six-hour process.

To make things easier for you, I precompiled OpenCV in Raspbian Jesse and created a downloadable image at `https://github.com/jcicolani/Jesse-OpenCV`.

You still need to walk through the installation and configuration process to customize the installation. The image includes the default settings that you need to change (with a few exceptions that were necessary to make the build).

The "Hard" Way

The more difficult method installs the Raspbian OS image directly on the SD card—ready to boot up. This is the method that I use because it really isn't any more complicated than the previous method, and it allows me to use versions that are not available through NOOBS.

You have two options for your Raspbian installation. Jessie is the most recent stable version of the operating system; it is what we'll be using. The first option is Raspbian Jessie with PIXEL—their new, optimized GUI. It is a 1.5GB download, and it is a 4.2GB image once it's been decompressed. The second option is Raspbian Jessie Lite, a minimal image that is a much smaller 300MB download (1.4GB after decompression). However, minimal means no GUI, so everything is done via the command line. If you're a fan of headless Linux, then this is the option for you. We will use the larger install with PIXEL.

If you have a BitTorrent client installed, click Download Torrent. This is much faster than downloading the .zip file.

1. Navigate to `www.raspberrypi.org/downloads/`.

2. Click the Raspbian image.

3. Select the Raspbian flavor that you want to install.

4. Once the download is complete, decompress the file somewhere that you'll easily find it.

5. Download and install Win32 Disk Imager. This allows you to write the image file that you just downloaded to the micro SD card. You can get it at `https://sourceforge.net/projects/win32diskimager/`.

6. Optionally, you may also want to download SDFormatter to make sure that your SD card is properly prepared. You can get it at `www.sdcard.org/downloads/formatter_4/`.

7. Insert your micro SD card into the card reader connected to your computer.

8. If you have downloaded and installed SDFormatter, open it. You should see a dialog box similar to the one shown in Figure 2-2.

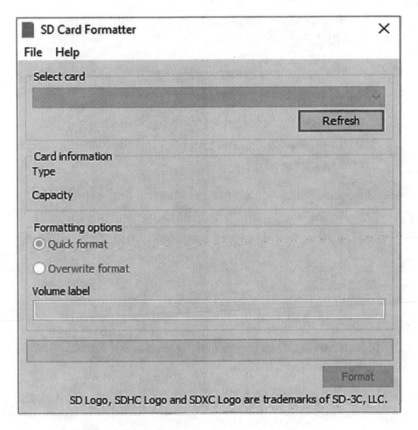

Figure 2-2. *SD Card Formatter*

9. Make sure that you select the drive representing
    your SD card. You're about to format it, so if you
    select the wrong thing, it will wipe out whatever you
    have on that drive. The tool usually selects the right
    one by default, but double check. It would be wise to
    disconnect any other external storage devices.

10. Make sure that **Format size adjustment** is set to **On**.
    This removes any other partitions on the card and
    uses the whole thing. Leave all the other settings at
    the default.

11.   Click **Start**. When the process finishes, you're ready to install the OS.

12.   To flash the image to the SD card, open Win32 Disk Imager.

13.   In the image file field, select the Raspbian image that you downloaded. You can click the file folder icon to navigate to it.

14.   Make sure that your SD card is selected in the device drop-down box. Again, selecting the wrong device can lead to a world of hurt; so pay attention.

15.   Click **Write**.

16.   Once the process has completed, remove the card from your card reader.

17.   Insert the card into the micro SD card reader on the Raspberry Pi.

That sounds lengthy, but it is remarkably fast and easy to do. Next, let's walk through the NOOBS installation process.

The "Easy" Way

I call this method the "easy" way, although the hard way is actually pretty easy. What makes this easy is that you don't have to write the image directly. You will probably want to format the card, but if it's a new card, that may not be necessary. To make it even easier, if you bought your Pi as part of a starter kit, it probably came with NOOBS already installed on a micro SD card. If this is the case, you can skip the first few steps.

You have two options: NOOBS and NOOBS Lite. NOOBS includes the Raspbian image with the download, so you won't have to connect to the network to download anything once it's on your SD card. You have the option of selecting another OS, if you so choose, but you'll need to have your Pi connected to the network for NOOBS to download it. NOOBS Lite does not include the full Raspbian image. For our purposes, select the standard NOOBS install.

1. Click the NOOBS image on the Downloads page.

2. Select your NOOBS flavor. If you have a BitTorrent client installed, click **Download Torrent**. This is much faster than downloading the .zip file.

3. Optionally, you may also want to download SDFormatter to make sure that your SD card is properly prepared. You can get it at www.sdcard. org/downloads/formatter_4/.

4. If you downloaded and installed SDFormatter, open it.

5. Make sure that you select the drive representing your SD card. You're about to format it, so if you select the wrong thing, it will wipe out whatever you have on that drive. The tool usually selects the right one by default, but double check. It would be wise to disconnect any other external storage devices.

6. Make sure that **Format size adjustment** is set to **On**. This removes any other partitions on the card and uses the whole thing. Leave all the other settings at the default.

7. Click **Start**. When the process has finished, you're ready to install the OS.

8. Unzip the NOOBS file directly onto the SD card.

9. Remove the card from your card reader.

10. Insert the card into the micro SD card reader on the Raspberry Pi.

11.   At this point, you need to hookup your Pi to continue. So, jump forward to the "Connecting Raspberry Pi" section in this chapter. Once you've complete those steps, come back to this section to continue the setup.

12.   When you connect power to the Raspberry Pi, it boots up to the NOOBS installation screen. If you used NOOBS Lite, you have your choice of OS. If you used the standard NOOBS download, your only option is Raspbian (which is OK because that's what we're using).

13.   Click **Raspbian** to make sure that it's selected. Also make sure that you select the correct language at the bottom of the screen (in my case, it is English (US)).

14.   Click the **Install** button at the top of the screen.

The installation could take a little while, so go ahead and grab a cup of coffee.

Connecting Raspberry Pi

Now that your micro SD card is ready to go, you need to hook up your Raspberry Pi. If you're using an original, first generation Pi, this is a little more complicated.

Every model after the original, however, includes multiple USB ports and an HDMI connector to make things easier. Hooking up the Pi is very simple.

1. Connect your monitor via the HDMI cable. If you are using a small television that is outfitted with component hookups rather than HDMI, the audio jack on the Pi is a four-pole component jack. You need an RCA-to-3.5mm converter, usually in cable form, to do this.

2. Connect your keyboard and mouse to the USB ports. I use a wireless keyboard/touchpad combination because it's compact and portable.

3. Make sure that your micro SD card with Raspbian or NOOBS is installed in the micro SD port on the Pi. Essentially, this is the hard drive for your small computer, so it has to be in the right place. It will not read the OS through an SD card reader connected to one of the USB ports.

4. If you are using an Ethernet cable, connect it to the Ethernet port. You may also plug a Wi-Fi dongle to the USB port. If you are using a Pi 3, as I am, Wi-Fi is built in.

5. Connect the 5V power to the micro USB port. This port is only for power. You cannot access the board via USB.

That's it. Your Raspberry Pi should look similar to what's shown in Figure 2-3. The Pi should be booting on your monitor. If you are installing NOOBS, go back to step 10 of the Noobian installation to complete the installation process.

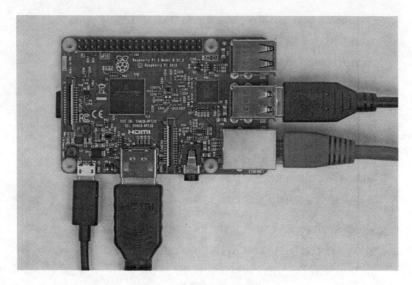

Figure 2-3. *Raspberry Pi connections*

Now that you're connected and booted up, you need to log in. The following are the default credentials for a Raspbian installation:

- Username: pi

- Password: raspberry

Of course, the default username and password are never secure. So, to keep your cybersecurity friends from running away with your robot, one of the first things we're going to do is change the password. Later in the configuration, we will change the default username.

Configuring Your Pi

Now that we've taken care of the initial installation, we're going to move on to a little customization. The Pi has several features that you can enable, depending on your particular use. Initially, they're not enabled to reduce some of the overhead needed to run the OS. The configuration settings that we're going to implement are for security and convenience.

Using raspi-config

To make customizations, the good folks at the Raspberry Pi Foundation have included a utility called *raspi-config*. A command-line terminal is necessary to use it. A single command is entered right now, but as we move forward in the workshops, you'll become much more familiar with the terminal window. If you're new to Linux (on which Raspbian is based), this can be a little intimidating. It doesn't need to be, and I'll do my best to ease you into it. But you will have to learn your way around it.

You can find more information about the raspi-config utility at www. raspberrypi.org/documentation/configuration/raspi-config.md.

At this point, you should have already booted into your Raspberry Pi. If not, do so now.

We will be doing several things to configure the Pi, starting with expanding the file system to take advantage of the entire SD card. By default, Raspbian doesn't use the entire SD card, so we'll want to tell it to. If you are using NOOBS, this has been done for you, so you can skip this step.

1. Click the Raspberry Pi icon at the top of the screen. This opens an application list.

2. Select **Accessories ➤ Terminal**, as shown in Figure 2-4. When opened, the terminal window is displayed (see Figure 2-5).

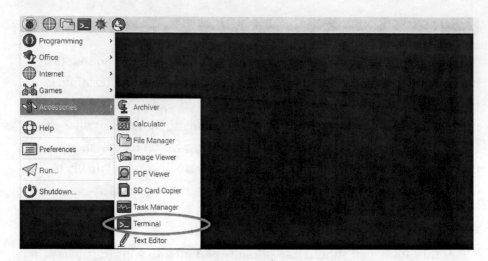

Figure 2-4. *Terminal selection from the applications list. The terminal icon is also on the quick access bar.*

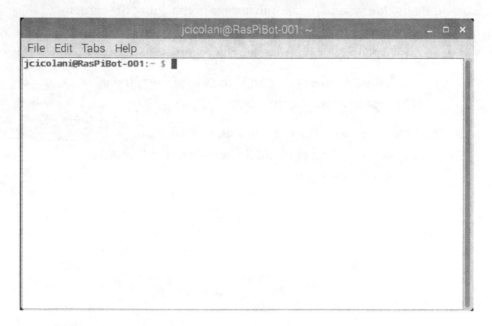

Figure 2-5. *Terminal window*

3. Type **sudo raspi-config**.

    This opens the Raspberry Pi Software Configuration
    Tool, as shown in Figure 2-6.

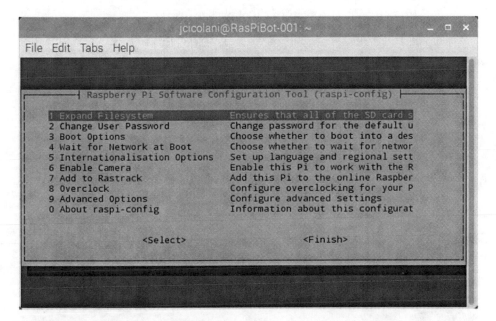

Figure 2-6.   *The raspi-config screen. Most OS-level options can be set
here, including activating and deactivating services.*

> Newer versions of Raspbian automatically expand
> your file system the first time you start the Pi. Unless
> you are using an older version of Raspbian, you
> should be able to skip this next step and move on to
> changing the password.

4. Make sure that **Expand file system** is highlighted.

5. Press Enter. The system pops up a message about
    expanding the file system and asks you to reboot.
    (We will reboot later, after we've made most of our
    changes.)

Next, we'll change the user password.

6.   Make sure that **Change user password** is highlighted.

7.   Press Enter. The system displays a message saying that you're going to be prompted for a new password.

8.   Press Enter. This drops you into the terminal to enter the new password.

9.   Enter your new password and press Enter.

10.   Confirm your new password and press Enter. This displays a confirmation that the password was successfully updated (see Figure 2-7).

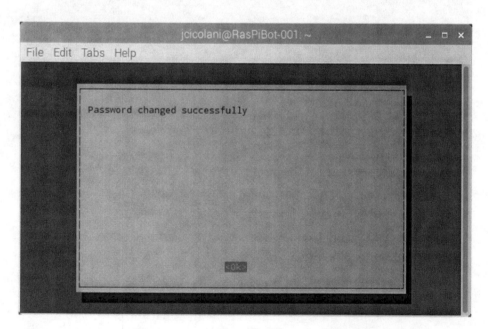

Figure 2-7. *A password change confirmation in raspi-config*

11. Press Enter.

The next few steps activate some services that we'll
be using later.

We'll start by changing the hostname of your Pi
to something unique that is easier to find on the
network. This becomes particularly important when
you're in a room with 20 other Raspberry Pis.

12. Make sure that advanced options is highlighted,
and then press Enter. This displays the interface and
other options (see Figure 2-8).

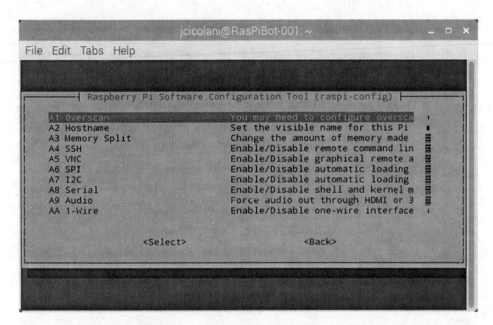

Figure 2-8. *raspi-config advanced options. Hostname and service
activation is accessed here.*

The hostname is how your Raspberry Pi appears on the network. You'll want to give your Pi a unique name, especially when you consider how many of them may be on the network at any given time. The hostname should be both meaningful to the application and unique.

13. Highlight **Hostname** and press Enter.

14. A dialog box explains the requirements for a hostname. It must be only alphanumeric characters: no symbols, no hyphens, and no underscores. Press Enter to continue.

15. Enter your new hostname and press Enter.

    SSH allows us to access the Pi through a terminal window (SSH client) from another computer. On Windows, PuTTY is a very popular, free SSH client. SSH does not provide a GUI. All interactions are made using terminal commands. This is helpful if you want to quickly execute a program, install software, and so forth. As you become more familiar with the terminal, you will likely find yourself using SSH to connect for simple commands, while reserving VNC (remote desktop) for more involved tasks such as writing programs.

16. Go back to the advanced options menu.

17. Select **Enable SSH** and press Enter.

18. Confirm that you want to enable SSH and press Enter.

19. Press Enter again to return to the menu.

I2C is a serial communications protocol that is very popular in embedded systems such as the Pi, Arduino, and so forth. It allows for robust communication with multiple devices by using a number of pins. The motor control board that we will use communicates via I2C. (If you later choose to add other boards, such as a servo control board, it will also use I2C.) As long as the devices have different addresses, you can keep stacking them.

20. Go back to the advanced options menu.

21. Select **Enable I2C** and press Enter.

22. Confirm that you want to enable SSH, and then press Enter.

23. Press Enter again to return to the menu.

    Because we also plan to use the Raspberry Pi headless (without a monitor, keyboard, or mouse attached), let's set it up to boot into the console automatically. Don't worry; it's easy enough to launch the desktop GUI when you want to, as you will see.

24. Go to boot options and press Enter.

25. Select **Console** and press Enter. If you trust that you'll be the only one accessing your Pi directly, you can choose **Console Autologin**. Autologin does not apply to remote sessions, just direct access with a keyboard and a monitor.

26. With all of the settings updated, highlight **Finish** and press Enter.

27.   The Pi asks if you want to reboot. Select **Yes** and press Enter.

At this point, your Pi reboots. This may take a few minutes, especially if you did not install via NOOBS and the Pi has to expand your file system.

Remember, we set up the Pi to boot into the console by default. Since the next few steps are all done via the command line, we'll not need to load the GUI. However, let's do it anyway so that you can see how easy it is.

28.   Type **startx** and press Return.

You're now in the GUI desktop.
To exit the desktop, do the following

1.   Click the programs menu (the raspberry in the upper-left corner).

2.   Click the power button.

3.   Select **Exit to command line**.

You should now be back to the command line.

Users

The default user on every installation of Raspbian is *pi*. Earlier, we changed the password to make it more secure. However, you probably don't want to always log on as the pi user.

Remember when I said we'd start using the terminal more? Well, that starts now. The easiest way to create and manage users is through the command line. We're going to walk through that process now.

Securing Root

In addition to the default user, pi, there is another default user on the Pi. This is the root user. The root user is, essentially, an administrative user that is used by the machine to execute low-level commands. This user has access to everything and can do anything because, well, it's the machine. Unlike the default pi user, however, root does not have a default password. It has no password.

So, while we're configuring and securing the computer for our robot, let's go ahead and give the root user a password.

1. Open a terminal window.

2. Type **sudo passwd root**. (Note that passwd is the proper command and not a typo.)

3. Enter the new password for the root user.

4. Enter the password again to confirm.

Your root user is now secured, which is good because you'll need it for the next step in the configuration.

Change the Default Username

The first thing you're going to do is change the default username to something of your choosing. What this will do is replace the username *pi* with your own username. This provides another layer of security on the device; now, not only would someone need to figure out the password, they wouldn't even have the default username to work with. It also preserves some of the special, undocumented permissions that the default user is given.

1. Log out of the pi user. You can do this through the menu system or by simply typing **logout** in a terminal.

2. Log on with your—now secure—root user.

3. Type

   usermod -l <newname> pi

   <newname> is the new username that you chose. Do
   not include < or > in the command.

4. To update the home directory name, type

   usermod -m -d /home/<newname> <newname>

   Again, <newname> is the new username that you
   used in the previous step.

5. Log out of the root user and log back in with your
   new username.

At this point, you have changed the default user credentials for both
the default user and the root user. You have also changed the hostname.
This is the minimum needed to secure your pi and your robot.

Your Raspberry Pi is now set up, configured, and ready for use. There
is one more thing we're going to want to do before we move on to the next
chapter, and that is setting up your Pi to be headless.

Making a machine "headless" simply means configuring it so you no
longer need to connect a monitor, a keyboard, and a mouse to it to operate
it. This is generally done in two ways: with a KVM switch or by setting
up remote access. On a mobile robot, connecting a KVM is not really an
option. In fact, it would be little different from simply having everything
connected to it. What we want to do is set up the Pi so that we can access it
remotely over the network. But first, let's make sure that you're connected
to your network.

Connecting to a Wireless Network

When you originally hooked up your Raspberry Pi, you had the option to connect an Ethernet cable. If you did this, then you are already on the network. You still want to connect to your wireless network, however. This allows you to remote into your robot while it's on the move. You'll be able to send it commands, update code, and even view the video feed from the webcam installed in Chapter 10.

To do connect to a wireless network, you need a Wi-Fi connection. If you're using a Raspberry Pi 3, then you already have one built in; otherwise, you need to get a Wi-Fi dongle, preferably one that can be powered by the USB port. A little research here goes a long way.

1. Log in to the GUI interface by typing **startx**.

2. Click the network icon at the top right of your screen. This icon looks like Figure 2-9.

Figure 2-9. *Network connection icon*

3. Select your wireless network from the list.

4. Enter the security key for your network.

You should now be connected to your wireless network.

Going Headless

You're not going to want to haul around an extra monitor, keyboard, and mouse while working through these workshops. To make your life much, much easier, let's set it up so you can access the Pi headless.

Remote Access

There are two ways to get remote access. One method is to use SSH, which allows you to connect to a remote device using a terminal client. The other method is to set up a remote desktop.

Remote Desktop with xrdp

Let's start with accessing the desktop remotely from another computer. The following instructions are for Windows users. Most modern Windows installations come with Remote Desktop Connection already installed, which is what we'll use to connect to the Pi once it's set up.

Let's install a couple of services on the Pi: tightVNCserver and xrdp. Theoretically, xrdp should install the VNC server all on its own. In actuality, it does not. At this point, you should be at the command line on your Pi.

1. Type **sudo apt-get install tightvncserver**.

2. Complete the installation.

3. Type **sudo apt-get install xrdp**.

    When the installation is complete, you should be ready to go.

To get connected, do the following.

4. On the Pi, type **sudo ifconfig**.

5. Note the Internet address (inet addr) in the eth0 block if you are using an Ethernet cable, or the wlan0 block for Wi-Fi.

6. On your laptop, open Remote Desktop Connection. This displays the connection dialog box, as shown in Figure 2-10.

Figure 2-10. *Windows Remote Desktop Connection*

7. Enter the inet addr from your Pi.

8. Click **Connect**.

    You should see the remote desktop screen with the
    xrdp login form (see Figure 2-11).

Figure 2-11. *XRDP remote desktop login screen*

9. Enter your username and password.

10. Click **OK**. This opens the desktop from your Pi
    (see Figure 2-12).

Figure 2-12. *Default Raspbian desktop viewed through a remote desktop session*

As long as the IP address of your Pi doesn't change, you no longer need the keyboard, mouse, or monitor to use your Pi.

SSH with PuTTY

The most common SSH client is probably PuTTY. It's free to use and can be downloaded from `www.chiark.greenend.org.uk/~sgtatham/putty/download.html`.

The file you downloaded for PuTTY is an executable, which won't need to be installed. Put it on your desktop or somewhere easy to find. To get connected, do the following.

1.   Open the PuTTY interface (see Figure 2-13).

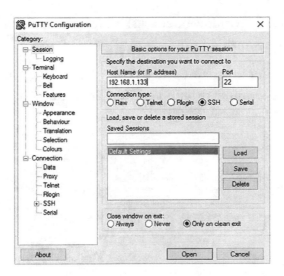

Figure 2-13. *PuTTY configuration window*

2. Enter your Raspberry Pi's IP address.

3. Click **Open**.

4. You will likely get a security warning, as shown in
    Figure 2-14, but we know that this is the proper
    connection, so click **Yes**.

Figure 2-14. *Security warning on first SSH connection with PuTTY*

A terminal window opens, asking for your username and password.

5. Enter your username and password. You should now see the terminal prompt, as shown in Figure 2-15.

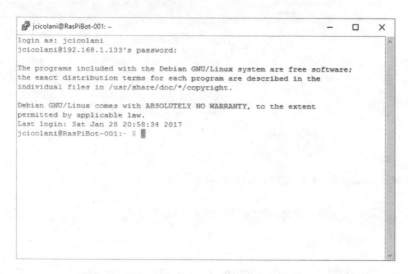

Figure 2-15. Open SSH connection

That's it. You are now connected via SSH to your Raspberry Pi. You can have multiple connections going at once, but don't have more than you need to. Multiple connections are handy when you're working with something like the Robot Operating System (ROS). (Don't worry, that's a ways away.) ROS runs multiple programs via the terminal. Each one requires its own terminal window. With PuTTY, you're able to have as many remote terminal connections as you need.

Finding Your Device on a Network

To access your Pi remotely, you need to know its IP address on the network. Generally, a network switch retains a device's IP from session to session; however, this isn't guaranteed.

Finding your device's IP address on the network can be tricky. If you are at home and have access to your router's admin panel, this is probably the most straightforward way to find your device. Simply log on to your router, find the list of connected devices, and scroll down until you find the hostname of your Raspberry Pi.

If you need to find the IP address but are away from home, there are a few ways to do it. The easiest is to use an Nmap app on your phone. I use an app called Fing on my Android phone. Once the phone is connected to the local Wi-Fi network, the app scans the network and lists all the other devices on that network. You can just scroll down the list until you find your hostname.

If the network is new to you, your Raspberry Pi will not automatically connect to it. This situation makes it a little tricky. To make things easier, be prepared before you go out. I am a Windows user; if you are not, you need to look up the proper procedure for your OS. I do this operation with the laptop I have when traveling. It allows me to remote into the Pi long enough to connect to the local Wi-Fi and get the wlan0 IP address.

Keep in mind that the IP is assigned by the laptop. The IP you get at the end of this operation will likely not work from any other machine.

On a Windows 7 or later machine, you can perform the following steps to remote into your Pi directly to get its IP address. Make note of the IP address should you ever need to connect directly to the Pi to set up a new Wi-Fi connection. You will need a short Ethernet cable, which should be added to your kit or toolbox.

Make sure that you are able to view your Raspberry Pi with a monitor, keyboard, and mouse set up, or through a remote connection via your Wi-Fi network. The Pi cannot be connected to the network via Ethernet cable because that port is needed for this operation.

1. Connect the Ethernet cable to your laptop.

2. Connect the other end to the Ethernet port on your Pi.

3. Open a terminal window on the Pi.

4. Type **sudo ifconfig**.

5. Locate the inet addr in the eth0 block.

6. Open a terminal window on your laptop. You can do this by searching `cmd` in the Start menu.

7. Type the following in the Windows terminal:

    ping <your.Pis.IP.address>

    `<your.Pis.IP.address>` is the eth0 IP address from your Pi.

8. Open Remote Desktop Connection on your laptop.

9. Enter the IP address from the Pi and press Enter.

You should now have a remote connection from your laptop directly to the Raspberry Pi. Make sure that you save this IP address where that you can find it later. Remote Desktop Connection should remember it, but it's a good idea to also save it somewhere else.

Now whenever you are trying to connect to a new Wi-Fi network, you can use the Ethernet cable to remote into your Pi directly from your laptop. Once remoted in, simply select the network from the list of available networks and enter the passcode, if there is one.

Summary

The Raspberry Pi was designed for the hobbyist maker. The small Linux computer makes it very useful for a lot of different types of projects, but this means that you need to learn a little Linux. The developers at the Raspberry Pi Foundation provide an easy to use a version of Debian Linux called Raspbian.

We took the basic installation a step further by configuring remote access. This allows you to remotely access your robot through your network, which means the monitor and keyboard are no longer needed.

Summary

CHAPTER 3

A Crash Course in Python

The purpose of this book is to challenge you to build a simple robot that is expanded over time. It is intended to be difficult. It is intended to provide a hands-on experience to help you past the most difficult part of learning robotics: being intimidated by the technology. I'm going to teach you some of the basics of robotics the same way that I learned how to swim— by being thrown in to the deep end while someone more experienced watches over to make sure that you don't drown.

So with that, I expect you to take what you experience and add to it through your own learning. I'll get you going in the right direction, but there's not going to be a lot of handholding. You have to fill in the gaps and learn some of the details—especially some of those for specific application—on your own.

This introduction to Python is no different. I am going to show you how to install the tools, use the editor, and write some simple programs. We are going to move quickly through program structure, syntax and formatting issues, data types, and variables, and right into control structures and some of the object-oriented aspects of Python. Don't worry if any of this sounds like techno-babble, you'll understand it before the end of this chapter.

© Jeff Cicolani 2018
J. Cicolani, *Beginning Robotics with Raspberry Pi and Arduino*,
https://doi.org/10.1007/978-1-4842-3462-4_3

At the end of the chapter, I don't expect you to be able to write your own programs. What I do expect is for you to know how to write code, to use and be comfortable with the editor, and to compile and execute programs. Most importantly, you should be able to look at someone else's code and be able to read it, have a basic understanding of what they are trying to do, and identify the building blocks. Dissecting other peoples' code is important to learning quickly. One premise of this book is to not reinvent the wheel. Most of what you're going to do has been done before, and it can be found if you do a little searching. Being able to read and understand what you find will help you reach your goals.

In term of resources, here's some advice:

- Community support for Python is excellent. The Python website is an invaluable source for learning and growing in Python. In particular, be sure to check out the beginner's page at `www.python.org/about/gettingstarted/`. We actually start here in the next section.

- Get yourself a good book or two on Python. This book gets you started, but there is a lot of detail that won't be covered. Look for books on design patterns in Python and different ways to build algorithms to make your code as efficient as possible. Find books that go in depth about your application.

- Don't think you have to learn Python, or any of the other topics in this book, on your own. There is an immense community out there. Find local meetups, clubs, and classes. Find your local hackerspace. I guarantee that you'll find someone there that is able to help you.

Python Overview

Python is a high-level programming language created by Guido van Rossum in the late 1980s. It has become a very popular general-purpose language because it's flexible, and relatively easy to learn and code. In many ways, Python is a very forgiving language, which lends to its ease of use. As you'll see later in this chapter, Python manages data in a manner that is very intuitive for people new to programming. As such, it is a very popular tool for teaching programming fundamentals. The peculiar way in which it uses variables to manage large data sets has also made it very popular in the growing field of data science. Data scientists can import volumes of data and perform operations on data sets with very little code. Of course, Python has peculiarities that we explore more in depth as we work through this chapter.

Downloading and Installing Python

First, let's discuss a little something about versions. There are essentially two flavors of Python: Python 2.7 and Python 3. In Python 3, creator Guido van Rossum decided to clean up the code without putting a lot of emphasis on backward compatibility; therefore, some of the code for version 2.7 simply won't work in version 3 and vice versa. Python 3 is the current version and everything will eventually move over to it. In fact, at this point, most everything has. In terms of robotics, the big holdout was OpenCV, an open source library of computer vision functions, which we'll use in Chapter 9. There are others that haven't fully migrated yet either, so you'll need to figure out what you want to do and if the packages you need have been ported over. We will use Python 2.7 for our project because many of the examples that you will find in your own research are in 2.7.

If you are using an Ubuntu or Debian Linux system, such as the Raspberry Pi, you're done. The Python tools are already installed and ready to go. Most Debian-based distributions install Python as part of the basic image.

If you are following along in Windows or another operating system, you need to install Python.

1. Navigate to `www.python.org/about/gettingstarted/`.

2. Click **Downloads**.

3. If you are using Windows, click **Download Python 2.7.13**.

4. If you're using another OS, select it from the list under **Looking for Python with a different OS?** This takes you to the appropriate download link.

5. If you want to use an older release of Python (for some bizarre reason), you'll find the appropriate links by scrolling down the page.

6. Once it's downloaded, run the installer and follow the directions on the screen.

Python Tools

There are numerous tools to support your Python development. Like most programming languages, the code is simply text that can be written with any text editor. You can write Python code with Notepad on your Windows machine. I wouldn't recommend it, but you can do it. Applications like Notepad++ recognize a Python script based on the file extension and then highlight the code accordingly.

Your options are quite extensive. However, for our exercises, we'll use the native tools that come with every installation of Python: the Python shell and the Python editor.

The Python Shell

The Python shell is an interface to the Python interpreter. Technically, if you're a fan of the command line, you could launch a terminal window and invoke the Python interpreter. However, we'll use the Python shell interface that is installed with Python, as shown in Figure 3-1. It provides a very clean interface for viewing and executing commands.

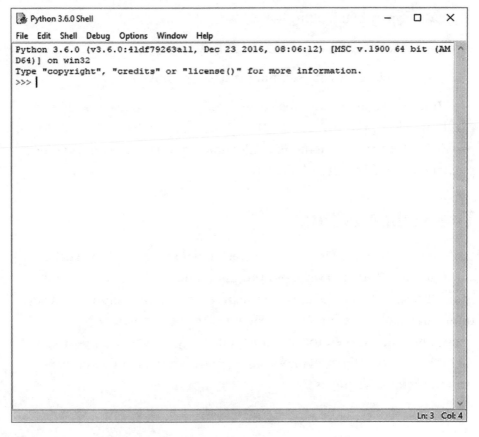

Figure 3-1. *The IDLE Python shell*

The Python shell is launched when you open the native IDLE IDE. Depending who you ask, IDLE either stands for *integrated development environment* or *integrated development and learning environment*. I like the latter simply because it makes more sense to me. But in essence, it's a windowed interface to the Python interpreter. It offers some features that you won't get in a simple command line.

- Simple editing features, such as find, copy, and paste

- Syntax highlighting

- A text editor with syntax highlighting

- A debugger with stepping and breakpoints

Since we'll use this interface a lot throughout the book, it would be prudent to learn more about the IDLE interface and the many tools that it provides. You can start at the IDLE documentation page at `https://docs.python.org/3/library/idle.html`.

The Python Editor

IDLE has another very important aspect: the text editor. We will use it throughout the book to write our programs and modules. The text editor is another aspect of IDLE and not a separate program, although it always opens in a separate window (see Figure 3-2). You can write Python programs in any text editor, and there are many IDEs that support Python. As I mentioned in the previous section, however, the IDLE interface provides a lot advantages.

Figure 3-2. *The IDLE file editor*

As you'll learn later, formatting is very important in Python. With other languages, such as C and Java, white space is irrelevant to the compiler. Spaces, tabs, new lines, and blank lines make the code more readable for people. In Python, however, indentation denotes code blocks. IDLE manages all of this for you. It automatically indents your code, reducing the likelihood of syntax errors due to improper indentation.

There are also several tools to help you with your code. For instance, as you type, IDLE presents a list of possible statements appropriate for where you are in a line. There are a few ways to invoke this feature. Many times, it automatically pops open while you are typing. This generally happens while you are inside a function call and there are only a limited number of possibilities. You can also force it open by hitting Ctrl-space while typing. When you do this, you see a list of possible statements to choose from. When you select one of these statements, it completes the word for you and presents you with other options if they are available, such as any appropriate parameters. These are called *calltips*.

Calltips display the expected values for an accessible function and open when you type " (" after the function name. It displays the function signature and the first line of the docstring. It remains open until the cursor is moved outside the function or the closing ") " is typed.

Context highlighting is done through colors. As you type your code, some of the words change color. The colors have meaning and are a quick, visual way to verify that you are on the right track. The contexts highlighted in this way are output, errors, user output and Python keywords, built-in class and function names, names following class and def, strings, and comments.

Let's see some of this in action.

1. Open IDLE.

2. Click **File ➤ New File**. This opens a new text editor window.

3. Type **pr**.

4. Press Ctrl-space. This displays the completion list with the word `print` highlighted.

5. Type **(**.

   This does a few things. It selects the highlighted text. In this case `print`. It also displays the calltip for the print function.

6. Type **"Hello World"**.

7. The calltip closes after you type the closing **)**.

8. Press Enter.

9. Save this file as `hello_world.py`.

10. Press F5 or select **Run ➤ Run Module** from the
    menu.

In the Python shell window, you should see something like this:

```
RESTART: D:/Projects/The Robot Group/Workshops/Raspberry Pi
Robot/hello_world.py
Hello World
```

If you see this, then your code was successful. If you received an error of some sort, go back to make sure that your code looks like this:

```
print("Hello World")
```

Oh, by the way, you just wrote and ran your first Python program. When compared to other languages, you'll notice Python's simplicity. Often, a few lines of a Python operation would take several more lines in C, C++, or Java.

The Zen of Python

Tim Peters, a long-time contributor to Python, wrote the governing principals behind Python development. I think it actually applies to all code and just about everything we do in robotics, and perhaps in life. They are tucked away as an Easter egg in the Python IDE.

1. Open IDLE.

2. Type **import this** and press Enter.

3. It should display the text shown in Figure 3-3
   (but do it anyway).

Figure 3-3. *The Zen of Python*

Writing and Running a Python Program

If you're following along as you should, then you've just written and run your first Python program. If you're not following along, don't worry, we'll do it again right now but with a little more programming.

Hello World

Let's add a simple variable call. We'll talk about variables in the very near future.

1. Open hello_world.py.

2. If you're one of those rebels I mentioned earlier, open IDLE.

3. Click **File ➤ New File**.

4. Save this file as hello_world.py.

    Now we're all on the same page...

5. Make the program look like this:

```
message = "Hello World"
print(message)
```

6. Save the file.

7. Press F5 or select **Run ➤ Run Module** from the menu.

You should see the same output as before:

```
RESTART: D:/Projects/The Robot Group/Workshops/Raspberry Pi
Robot/hello_world.py
Hello World
```

All we did here was move the text from the print function into a variable, and then told Python to print the contents of that variable. I'll cover variables shortly.

Basic Structure

Before we begin looking at program specifics, we need to be familiar with the structure of a Python program. We'll take a look at the different parts of a program, how the program is formated using indentation, and how you will add meaningful context using comments.

Program Parts

As you've seen, there aren't many required parts for a Python program. Most programing languages require you to create, at the very least, a main function of some sort. For the Arduino it is the `loop()` function. In C++, it is `main()`. Python does not have that. It jumps right into executing whatever commands it finds as it steps through the file. However, this does not mean that it's entirely linear. I discuss functions and classes later in the workshop, but just know that the interpreter scans through the file and builds whatever functions and classes it finds before executing the other commands. This is one of the things that make Python so easy to learn. It simply doesn't have quite as rigid of framework as you would find in most other languages.

Oh, and for you programming language purists, Python walks the line between a scripting language, where everything is executed through the interpreter, and a programming language. Some of the code is compiled into executables like C and C++. In fact, as we start to build modules, this is exactly what happens. However, in this book, we usually run it through the interpreter.

Indentation

As we work through the workshop, our programs become more complex. In particular, we're going to start working with code blocks, which are commands that are grouped together to execute in a function or a loop, or as part of a condition. This kind of structure is critical to writing effective programs.

All programming languages have syntax for formatting code blocks. C-based languages, including Java, use curly brackets {} to contain a code block. Python does not do this. Python uses indentation. Blocks of code are indented to indicate that they are a related block. If a line in a block is not properly indented, you'll get an error. This is one of the key reasons that we use IDLE. It automatically manages indentations. That doesn't mean that you, as a user, can't botch the program; it just means this type of error is greatly reduced.

As we progress through the workshop, you'll see the importance of indentation. In the meantime, just know it's important.

Finally, I want to make a brief note about indentation and editors. Text editors use different forms of indentation. Some use tab characters while others use two or four spaces. You are not able to see what is being used because these are invisible characters. This causes no end of frustration when you move from one editor to another. The better editors allow you to choose how you want the tab key to work (with a tab character or with a number of spaces, usually four). By default, IDLE uses four spaces.

Comments

Commenting code has become more important over time. It is an area where programmers are notoriously deficient. They use comments, but they are frequently cryptic or make assumptions about knowledge of the program that may not hold true for someone who picks up the code later. This would be less of an issue if they were any better about other forms of documentation. But, alas, they are not.

My lamentations aside, commenting is important, especially as you're learning. So, get into the habit of using comments. Use them to explain what you're doing or to enter small notes regarding logic.

A comment in Python is any line that begins with #. Python ignores everything following the # to the end of the line; for example:

```
# create a variable to hold the text
message = "Hello World"

# print the text stored in the variable
print(message)
```

In the preceding code, I added two comment lines to our hello_world.py program. I also added a blank line to help make the code a little easier to read. If you were to save and run this program, you would get exactly the same output that you did before.

You can also create a comment block using triple quotation marks, """. The Python compiler ignores any code between sets of these marks. You open and close the block with them. This allows you to write as much information as you'd like over multiple lines. This notation is frequently used for title blocks at the beginning of a file.

```
"""
Hello World
the simplest of all programs
By: Everyone who has written a program, ever
"""
```

It is a good habit to simply outline your code with comments before you write it. Before you start writing, think about what you need your code to do and how you will go about doing it. Create a flow chart or simply write down the steps that you will take to accomplish your goal. Then translate this into a series of comments in your file before you write any actual code. This helps you structure the problem in your mind and improves your overall flow. If you identify a step that you are repeating, you likely have a candidate for a function. If you find that you are referencing a structured concept (like robot) that you want to imbue with special properties and functionality, you've got a class. Later, I discuss functions and classes in further detail.

Running a Program

As you saw earlier, there are a few ways to run a Python program.

From IDLE, you can simply press F5. You'll need to make sure that the file is saved first, but this runs your file. If the file is not saved, you are prompted to do so. It is the same as selecting **Run ➤ Run Module** from the menu bar.

If your system is properly configured to run Python from the command line, you can execute a program from there, as well. You'll need to either navigate to the location of the file or have the full file location in the call. To execute a Python script from the command line, you type python followed by the file to be run.

```
> python hello_world.py
> python c:\exercises\hello_world.py
> python exercises\hello_world.py
```

All three of these commands would run our Hello World program, although two of them are operating system specific. The first command assumes that you are executing the file from within the directory it is stored. The second command runs the program in Windows, assuming it is saved within a folder called exercises on the root of the C:\ drive. The third command runs the program on a Linux machine, assuming the file is saved in a file called exercises in your home directory.

Programming in Python

In the next few sections, we use the Python shell and enter commands directly. A little later, we get back to writing program files. But, for now, everything we're doing can be demonstrated in the shell window.

Variables

Variables are essentially a convenient container for storing information. In Python, variables are very flexible. You don't need to declare a type. The type is generally determined when you assign a value to it. In fact, you declare a variable by assigning a value to it. This is important to remember when you start with numbers. In Python, there is a difference between 1 and 1.0. The first number is an integer and the second number is a float. More on that shortly.

Here are some general rules for variables:

- They can only contain letters, numbers, and underscores

- They are case sensitive; for example, `variable` is not the same as `Variable`. That's going to bite you later.

- Don't use Python keywords

In addition to these hard-and-fast rules, here are a couple of tips:

- Make the variable name meaningful with as few characters as possible

- Be careful when using lowercase L and uppercase O. These characters look very similar to 1 and 0, which can lead to confusion. I'm not saying don't use them; just make sure that it's clear what you're doing. It is strongly discouraged to use them as single-character variable names.

Data Types

Python is a dynamically typed language. This means that the type of data stored in a variable is not checked until the program is being executed, not while it is being compiled. This allows you to postpone assigning a type until a value is assigned. However, Python is also strongly typed, and it will fail if you try to perform an operation that is not valid for that data type. For instance, you cannot perform mathematical operations on a variable containing a string. As such, it is important to keep track of what type of data your variable references.

I'm going to talk about two basic data types: strings and numbers. Then I'll discuss some of the more complex types: tuples, lists, and dictionaries. Python allows you to define your own types as classes. I'll cover classes toward the end of the chapter, since there are a few other concepts we need to cover first.

Strings

A *string* is a collection of one or more characters contained within quotes. Quotes are how you indicate a string. For instance, "100" is a string; 100 is a number (an integer to be more accurate). You can use double or single quotation marks (just remember what you used). You can nest one type of quotes within another, but you will get an error, or worse, unexpected results, if you cross your quotes.

Here's an example of double quotes:

```
>>>print("This is text")
This is text
```

Here's an example of single quotes:

```
>>>print('This is text')
This is text
```

Here's an example of single quotes inside double quotes:

```
>>>print("'This is text'")
'This is text'
```

Here's an example of double quotes inside single quotes:

```
>>>print('"This is text"')
"This is text"
```

Triple quotes are used to span multiple lines within a string.

Here's an example of triple quotes:

```
>>>print("""this
is
text""")
this
is
text
```

You can use single quotes as apostrophes if you escape them first. Escaping a character simply means you are telling the interpreter to view a character as a string character rather than a functional one.

Here's an example of escaping quotes:

```
>>>print('This won't work')
File "<stdin>", line 1
        print('this won't work')
                  ^
SyntaxError: invalid syntax

>>>print('This won\'t error')
This won't error
```

You can do this to the entire string by making it a *raw string*. In this next example, '/n' is used to move to a new line.

Here's an example of a raw string:

```
>>>print('something\new')
something
ew
```

```
>>>print(r'something\new')
something/new
```

String Manipulation

There are a lot of ways to manipulate strings. Some are fairly straightforward, such as concatenation—adding strings together. However, some of them are a little surprising. Strings are treated as a list of character values. Later in this chapter, we explore lists in greater detail. However, we are going to use some of the traits of lists to work with strings.

Because strings are lists, which are similar to arrays in other languages, we can reference specific characters within a string. Like lists, strings are zero indexed. This means the first character of a string is at position zero.

With strings, like lists, the first character is at index [0]:

```
>>>robot = 'nomad'
>>>robot[0]
n
```

When using a negative number, the index begins at the end of the string and works backward.

```
>>>robot[-1]
t
```

Slicing a string allows you to extract a substring. When slicing a string, you provide two numbers separated by a colon. The first number is the starting index and the second is the ending index.

```
>>>robot[0:3]
nom
```

Note that when slicing, the first index is inclusive and the second index is exclusive. In the previous example, the value at index [0] returned, "r"; whereas the value at index [3] was not, "o".

When slicing, if you leave one of the indexes, the beginner or the end of the string is assumed.

```
>>>robot[:3]
nom
```

```
>>>robot[3:]
ad
```

Adding strings together is called *concatenation*. With Python, you can easily add strings together. This works with string literals and string variables. You can also multiply strings for an interesting effect.

You can add two strings together.

```
>>>print("Ro" + "bot")
Robot
```

You can add string variables together, like this:

```
>>>x = "Ro"
>>>y = "bot"
>>>z = x + y
>>>print(z)
Robot
```

You can add a string variable and literal.

```
>>>print(x + "bot")
Robot
```

You can multiply string literals.

```
>>>print(2 * "ro" + "bot")
rorobot
```

The multiplication of strings, however, only works on literals. It won't work on string variables.

I suggest spending some time exploring these and other string manipulation methods. For more information, go to `https://docs.python.org/3/tutorial/introduction.html#strings` and `https://docs.python.org/3.1/library/stdtypes.html#string-methods`.

Numbers

Numbers in Python come in a few flavors, the most common of which are integers and floats. An integer is a whole number, whereas a float is a decimal. Python also uses a Boolean type that has a value of one or zero. These are frequently used as a flag or state, where one means "on" and zero means "off." A Boolean is a subclass of integers and are treated as integers when performing operations.

As you might expect, you can perform mathematical operations with number types. Generally, if you perform arithmetic with one type, the result is that type. Math using integers usually results in an integer. However, if you perform division with integers, the result is a float. Math with floats result in a float. If you perform arithmetic with both types, the result is a float.

Adding two integers results in an integer.

```
>>>2+3
5
```

Adding two floats result in a float.

```
>>>0.2+0.3
0.5
```

Adding a float and an integer results in a float.

```
>>>1+0.5
1.5
```

Subtraction and multiplication work the same way.

```
>>>3-2
1

>>>3-1.5
1.5

>>>2*3
6

>>>2*0.8
1.6
```

Division always results in a float.

```
>>>3.2/2
1.6

>>>3/2
1.5
```

The ** operator results in the first number raised to the power of the second.

```
>>>3**2
9
```

There is one catch with Python floats, however. The interpreter sometimes produces a seemingly arbitrary number of decimal places. This has to do with how floating-point notation is stored in Python and how math is done within the interpreter.

```
>>>0.2+0.1
0.30000000000000004
```

For more information about this anomaly, go to https://docs. python.org/3/tutorial/floatingpoint.html.

Lists

A *list* is a collection of items in a particular order. In other languages, they are generally known as *arrays*. You can put anything you want in a list. The values stored in a list don't have to be of the same data type. However, if you mix data types in a list, make sure that you know which type you are getting when you use it.

You worked with lists when you worked with strings. A string is essentially a list of characters. As such, indexing and slicing work with lists, as well.

A list is created using square brackets [].

```
>>> robots = ["nomad","Ponginator","Alfred"]
>>> robots
['nomad', 'Ponginator', 'Alfred']
```

Like strings, lists are zero indexed. This means the first element in a list is at position 0, the second is at position 1, and so forth. You can access the individual elements of a list by calling its index or location within the list.

```
>>>robots[0]
'nomad'
```

```
>>>robots[-1]
'Alfred'
```

Lists can also be sliced. When a list is sliced, the result is a new list containing the subset of the original list.

```
>>>robots[1:3]
['Ponginator','Alfred']
```

It is easy to add, change, and remove members of a list using slicing and concatenation.

This example adds members to a list.

```
>>>more_bots = robots+['Roomba','Neato','InMoov']
>>>more_bots
['nomad', 'Ponginator', 'Alfred', 'Roomba', 'Neato', 'InMoov']
```

This example changes members in a list.

```
>>>more_bots[3] = 'ASIMO'
>>>more_bots
['nomad', 'Ponginator', 'Alfred', 'ASIMO', 'Neato', 'InMoov']
```

This example removes the members of a list.

```
>>>more_bots[3:5] = []
>>>more_bots
['nomad', 'Ponginator', 'Alfred', 'InMoov']
```

Assign list members to variables:

```
>>>a,b = more_bots[0:2]
>>>a
'nomad'
>>>b
'Ponginator'
```

There are a number of methods automatically included in lists. For example, you can force the first letter of a name to be capitalized.

```
>>> print(robots[0].title())
Nomad
```

As I mentioned, a list can contain any type of data, including other lists. In fact, when we start working with computer vision, we will frequently use lists of lists to hold image data.

Lists are a very powerful and important aspect of Python. Visit https://docs.python.org/3/tutorial/introduction.html#lists to spend some time exploring lists.

Tuples

You're going to hear the term *tuple* a lot when working with Python. A tuple is simply a special kind of list that cannot be changed. Think of a tuple as a list of constants, or a constant list. You declare a tuple using parentheses rather than square brackets.

Tuples are immutable, which means that once a tuple has been created, it cannot be changed. To change the contents of a tuple, a new tuple must be created. This is done using the same slicing techniques we used for strings and lists.

```
>>> colors = ("red","yellow","blue")
>>> colors
('red', 'yellow', 'blue')
>>>colors2 = colors[0:2]
>>>colors2
('red','yellow')
```

Note that we used list notation when slicing the tuple, colors[0:2] rather than colors(0:2). The result of the slice is still a tuple.

A tuple, however, can be replaced.

```
>>>colors2 = (1,2,3)
>>>colors2
(1,2,3)
```

They can also be replaced with an empty tuple.

```
>>>colors2 = ()
>>>colors2
()
```

Dictionaries

A *dictionary* is similar to a list except that it allows you to name your items in the list. This is done using key/value pairs. The key becomes the index for the value. This allows you to add some meaningful structure to your lists. They are useful for holding a list of parameters or properties.

A dictionary is declared using curly brackets rather than square brackets.

```
>>> Nomad = {'type':'rover','color':'black','processor':'Jetson
TX1'}
>>> print(Nomad['type'])
Rover
```

You work with dictionaries in much the same way as you would an array. Except rather than providing an index number, you provide the key to access an element.

There are a couple of things to know about dictionaries before you use them.

- The key must be an immutable value, such as a number or a string. Tuples can also be used as keys.

- A key cannot be defined more than once in a dictionary. Like variables, the value of a key is the last one assigned.

```
>>>BARB = {'type':'test-bed','color':'black','type':'wheeled'}
>>>BARB
{'color':'black','type':'wheeled'}
```

- In this example, the first 'type' value was overwritten by the second one.

- Dictionaries can be nested as values within other dictionaries. In the following example, I have embedded the definition for my ongoing robotics project, Nomad into a dictionary of my robots.

```
>>>myRobots = {'BARB':'WIP','Nomad':Nomad,'Llamabot':'WIP'}
>>>myRobots
{'BARB': {'color':'black','type':'wheeled'},'Nomad': {'color':'
black','type':'wheeled'},'Llamabot':'WIP'}
```

Of course, a dictionary wouldn't be all that useful if you weren't able to update and manipulate the values contained within. Making changes to a dictionary is similar to making changes to a list. The only real difference is that you use the key rather than the position to access the various elements.

To update a value, use the key to reference the value to be changed.

```
>>>myRobots['Llamabot'] = 'Getting to it'
>>>myRobots
{'BARB': {'color':'black','type':'wheeled'},'Nomad': {'color':'
black','type':'wheeled'},'Llamabot':'Getting to it'}
```

A key/value pair can be removed with the del statement.

```
>>>del myRobots['Llamabot']
>>>myRobots
{'BARB': {'color':'black','type':'wheeled'},'Nomad': {'color':'
black','type':'wheeled'}}
```

A dictionary can be copied with the copy method of the dictionary class. To access the copy method, start with the name of the dictionary and add .copy() to the end.

```
>>>workingRobots = myRobots.copy()
>>>workingRobots
{'BARB': {'color':'black','type':'wheeled'},'Nomad': {'color':'
black','type':'wheeled'}}
```

To append one dictionary to the end of another, use the update method.

```
>>>otherRobots = {'Rasbot-pi':'Pi-bot from
book','spiderbot':'broken'}
>>>myRobots.update(otherRobots)
>>>myRobots
{'BARB': {'color':'black','type':'wheeled'},'Nomad':
{'color':'black','type':'wheeled'},'Rasbot-pi':'Pi-bot from
book','spiderbot':'broken'}
```

None Type

There is a special data type that is very important when working with classes and objects imported from other sources. This is the *none type*, which is an empty placeholder. It is used when we want to declare an object but define it later. It is also used to empty an object. You will see the none type in action later in this chapter, when we discuss classes. In the meantime, know that it exists and that it is essentially an empty placeholder.

A Final Note on Variables

As you worked through the examples in this section, you were working with variables. Notice how a variable accepted whatever value you provided it and happily returned exactly what you assigned. If you assign a list to a variable, it returns the list—square brackets and all. The same holds true for tuples, dictionaries, strings, and numbers. Whatever you assign to it is exactly what you get back. We saw this in action when we nested one dictionary inside another. By simply adding the dictionary name into the definition of another, we embedded all the values into the new dictionary.

Why do I point this out?

Later in the book, when we start working with functions and classes, you will assign complex data structures to your variables. It is important to know that whatever you assign to a variable is what the variable contains, and you can apply any methods or functions appropriate for that data type.

```
>>> robots = ["nomad","Ponginator","Alfred"]
>>> robots
['nomad', 'Ponginator', 'Alfred']
>>> myRobot = robots[0]
>>> myRobot
'nomad'
>>> myRobot.capitalize()
'Nomad'
```

We used a method of the String class on our string variable, myRobot. A method is functionality that we give to a class. Since a data type is a built-in class, we can use methods from that class on our variables. I'll discuss methods in much more detail when we start working with classes toward the end of this chapter.

Control Structures

In this section, we're going to explore how to add structure to your code. Rather than just stepping through a program and executing each line of code as it is encountered, you probably want more control. These control structures allow you to execute code only when a specific condition exists, and to perform blocks of code multiple times.

For the most part, it's going to be easier to walk you through these concepts than trying to describe them.

if Statements

The if statement allows you to test for a condition before you execute a block of code. The condition can be any value or equation that evaluates to either true or false.

This next piece of code loops through the robots list and determines whether the robot is Nomad.

```
>>> for robot in robots:
        if robot=="Nomad":
                print("This is Nomad")
        else:
                print(robot + " is not Nomad")

This is Nomad
Ponginator is not Nomad
Alfred is not Nomad
```

Again, note the indentation as you type. IDLE indents another level after each line that ends in a colon, which should be every line that denotes a new block, such as loop statements and conditionals.

It's important to also note how we test for equality. A single equals sign means assignment. Double equals signs tell the interpreter to compare for equality.

```
>>> myRobot = "Nomad"
>>> myRobot == "Ponginator"
False
>>> myRobot == "Nomad"
True
```

Here is a list of comparators:

Equals	==
Not equal	!=
Less than	<
Greater than	>
Less than or equal to	<=
Greater than or equal to	>=

You can also use and and or to test for multiple conditions.

```
>>> for robot in robots:
        if robot == "Ponginator" or robot == "Alfred":
                print("These aren't the droids I'm looking for.")

These aren't the droids I'm looking for.
These aren't the droids I'm looking for.
```

Comparisons are also frequently used to determine if an object exists or contains a value. Essentially, a condition evaluates to true if it does not evaluate to false, 0, or none. This is very handy when you want to execute a piece of code only if an object exists, such as when you initialize sensors or connections through a serial port or network.

Loops

When you work with robotics, there are times that you want to repeat a block of code. Whether to perform a set of instructions on a collection of objects, or to execute a block of code for long as a condition exists, you need to use a loop.

Loops allow you to repeat a block of code to perform the tasks multiple times. There are two flavors of loops: the for loop and the while loop. Each provides a specific functionality that is crucial to writing efficient programs.

for Loop

A `for` loop performs a block of code for each element in a list. A collection of values— a tuple, list, or dictionary—is provided to the `for` loop. It then iterates through the list and executes the code contained in the code block. When it runs out of elements in the collection, the loop is exited and the next line of code outside the `for` block is executed.

As with the `if` statement, you put the code you want to run as part of the loop into a block indicated by indentation. It is important to make sure that you have your indentation correct, or you will get an error.

As you enter this into the Python shell, pay attention to what it does with indentation.

After you've entered the `print` command and pressed Enter, you need to press Enter again so that the shell knows that you're done.

```
>>> for robot in robots:
        print(robot)

Nomad
Ponginator
Alfred
```

The program enters the robots list and pulls the first value, Nomad, which it then prints. Since this is the last line in the block, the interpreter returns to the list and extracts the next value. This repeats until there are no more values in the list. At this time, the program exits the loop.

I tend to use plural words for my list names. This allows me to use the singular form of the name to reference items within the list for a loop. For instance, each element in the tuple of Robots is a robot.

If you want to loop through the elements in a dictionary, you want to provide two variables to store the individual elements. You also need to use the `items` method of the dictionary class. This allows you to access each key/value pair in turn.

```
>>>for name,data in Nomad.items():
        print(name + ': ' + data)
```

```
color: black
type: wheeled
```

You can use the enumerate function to add a sequential numeric value to the output of a for loop.

```
>>>for num,robot in enumerate(robots):
        print(num,robot)
```

```
(0, 'Nomad')
(1, 'Ponginator')
(2, 'Alfred')
```

while Loop

Whereas a for loop executes a block of code for each element in a list, the while loop executes a block of code as long as its condition evaluates to true. It is often used to execute code a specific number of times or while the system is in a specific state.

To loop through code a specific number of times, you use a variable to hold an integer value. In the following example, we tell the program to run the code for as long as the value of our count variable is less than five.

```
>>> count = 1
>>> while count < 5:
        print(count)
        count = count+1
```

```
1
2
3
4
```

We start by declaring a variable, count, to hold our integer, and we assign it the value 1. We enter the loop and the value of 1 is less than 5, so the code prints the value to the console. We then increment the value of count by 1. Because this is the last statement in the loop, and the last value evaluated by the while condition was less than 5, the code returns to the while clause. The value of count, now 2, is still less than 5, so the code executes again. This process repeats until the value of count is 5. Five is not less than five, so the interpreter exits the loop without executing the code in the block.

Had we forgotten to increment the count variable, it would have resulted in an open loop. Because count is equal to 1, and we never increment it, the value of count is always equal to 1. One is less than five, so the code would never stop executing and we would need to press Ctrl-C to end it.

It's also used as a type of main loop, executing the code continuously. You see the following in a lot of programs:

```
while(true):
```

True always evaluates to true; therefore, the code within this block keeps executing until the program is exited. This is called an *open loop* since there is no close to it. Fortunately, there is a convenient way to exit open loops. If you find yourself in an open loop, or you just want to exit a program arbitrarily, press Ctrl-C. This causes the program to exit immediately. You will use this frequently.

This technique can also be used to make the program wait for a specific condition to be met. For instance, if we required a serial connection to be available before we continued, we would first initiate the connection command. Then we could wait for the connection to complete before continuing by using some like this:

```
while(!connected):
        pass
```

The exclamation mark, also called a *bang*, represents *not*. So, in this case, assuming the `connected` variable contains the serial connection that evaluates to true when it is established, we are telling the program to execute the code contained in the `while` block as long as it is not connected.

In this case, the code we tell it to execute is called a *pass*, which is an empty command. It is used when you don't actually want to do anything, but you need something there. So, we are telling the system this: "While you're not connected, don't do anything, and loop until you are connected."

Functions

Functions are predefined blocks of code that we can call from within the program to perform a task. We've been using the `print()` function throughout this chapter. The `print()` command is a built-in function in Python. There are many predefined functions in Python and many more that can be added using modules. For more information about the available functions, check out the Python Standard Library at `https://docs.python.org/3/library/index.html`.

There will be many times that you want to create your own functions. Functions serve a few purposes.

Most often, you use a function to contain code that you want to execute throughout your program. Anytime you find yourself repeating the same set of operations throughout your code, you have a likely candidate for a function.

Functions are also widely used as a form of housekeeping. They can be used to move long processes somewhere other than your main program. This can make your code much easier to read. For instance, you could define actions for your robot as functions. When a condition is met in your main code, you simply call that function. Compare these two blocks of pseudo code:

```
while(true):
        if command==turnLeft:
```

```
        /*
        Lengthy list of instructions to turn left
        */
    if command==turnRight:
        /*
            Lengthy list of instructions to turn right
        */
    /* etc. */
```

And

```
while(true):
    if command==turnLeft:
        turnLeft()
    if command==turnRight:
        turnRight()
    /* etc. */
```

In the first block, the code to move the robot is contained in the if statement. If it takes 30 lines of code to turn left (not likely, but bear with me), your main code would be 30 lines longer. If turning right takes the same amount of code, you would have another 30 lines—all of which you have to go through to find the line you are looking for. This gets very tedious.

In the second block, the code to turn is moved to a separate function. This function is defined elsewhere in the program, or as you'll learn when we discuss libraries and modules, it could live in another file. This makes it easier to write and to read.

Defining a Function

To define your own function, you create the name of the function and a block of code that contains the operations you want to perform. The definition starts with the def keyword, followed by the name of the function, parentheses, and a colon.

Let's create a simple function:

```
>>> def hello_world():
        message = "Hello World"
        print(message)
>>> hello_world()
Hello World
```

In this code, we created a simple function that simply prints the message "Hello World". Now, whenever we want to print that message, we simply call that function.

```
>>> hello_world()
Hello World
```

To make things a little more interesting, we can provide the function with data to use. These are called *arguments*.

Passing Arguments

Frequently, we want to give information to the function to work with or on. To provide the information, we give the function one or more variables in which to store this information, called arguments.

Let's create a new function that greets the user.

```
>>> def hello_user(first_name, last_name):
        print("Hello " + first_name + " " + last_name + "!")
>>> hello_user("Jeff","Cicolani")
Hello Jeff Cicolani!
```

Here we created a new function called hello_user. We told it to expect to receive two pieces of information: the user's first name and last name. The variable names in the function definition contain the data we want to use. The function simply prints the greeting using the two arguments that we provide.

Default Values

You can create a default value for an argument by simply assigning a value as you declare the function.

```
>>> def favorite_thing(favorite = "robotics"):
        print("My favorite thing in the world is "+ favorite)
>>> favorite_thing("pie")
My favorite thing in the world is pie
>>> favorite_thing()
My favorite thing in the world is robotics
```

Note that the second time we called the function, we did not include a value. So, the function simply used the default value we assigned when we created the function.

Return Values

Sometimes we don't just want the function to do something on its own. Sometimes we want it to give a value back to us. This is helpful to move a common calculation to a function, or if we want the function to validate that it ran correctly. Many built-in functions and those from external libraries return a 1 if the function succeeded and 0 if it failed.

To return a value, simply use the return keyword followed by the value or variable that you want to return. Keep in mind that return exits the function and provides the value to the line that called the function. So, make sure that you don't do anything after the return statement.

```
>>> def how_many(list_of_things):
        count = len(list_of_things)
        return count
>>> how_many(robots)
3
```

A `return` statement can return more than one value. To return more than one value, separate each one with a comma. The function puts the values into a tuple that can be parsed by the calling code.

```
>>> def how_many(list_of_things):
        count = len(list_of_things)
        return count, 1

>>> (x, y) = how_many(robots)
>>> x
3
>>> y
1
```

Adding Functionality through Modules

Modules are essentially a collection of functions in a file that you can include in your program. There are countless modules to make your life easier. Many modules are included as part of the standard Python installation. Others are available for download from various developers. If you can't find what you're looking for, you can create your own custom modules.

Importing and Using Modules

Importing modules is easy. As you've seen, you simply use the `import` keyword followed by the name of the module. This loads all the functions of that module for your use. Now, to use one of the functions from the module, you need to enter the module name followed by the function.

```
>>> import math
>>> math.sqrt(9)
3.0
```

Some packages are very large, and you may not want to import the entire thing. If you know the specific function you need in your program, you can import only that part of the module.

This imports the `sqrt` function from the math module. If you import just the function, you will not need to prefix the function with the module name.

```
>>> from math import sqrt
>>> sqrt(9)
3.0
```

Lastly, you can provide an alias for the modules and functions that you import. This becomes very handy when you import a module with a fairly long name. In this example, I'm just being lazy:

```
>>> import math as m
>>> m.sqrt(9)
3.0
>>> from math import sqrt as s
>>> s(9)
3.0
```

Built-in Modules

The core Python libraries provide a lot of functionality for basic programs. However, there is a lot more functionality available, written by other developers and researchers. But before we go off into the wonderful world of third-party modules, let's look at what comes with Python.

Open an IDLE instance and type the following:

```
>>> import sys
>>> sys.builtin_module_names
```

You should get output that looks something like this:

```
('_ast', '_bisect', '_codecs', '_codecs_cn', '_codecs_hk',
'_codecs_iso2022', '_codecs_jp', '_codecs_kr', '_codecs_tw',
'_collections', '_csv', '_datetime', '_functools', '_heapq',
'_imp', '_io', '_json', '_locale', '_lsprof', '_md5',
'_multibytecodec', '_opcode', '_operator', '_pickle',
'_random', '_sha1', '_sha256', '_sha512', '_signal', '_sre',
'_stat', '_string', '_struct', '_symtable', '_thread',
'_tracemalloc', '_warnings', '_weakref', '_winapi', 'array',
'atexit', 'audioop', 'binascii', 'builtins', 'cmath', 'errno',
'faulthandler', 'gc', 'itertools', 'marshal', 'math', 'mmap',
'msvcrt', 'nt', 'parser', 'sys', 'time', 'winreg', 'xxsubtype',
'zipimport', 'zlib')
```

This is a list of the modules that are built into Python and are available for use right now.

To get more information about a module, you can use the help() function. It lists all the modules currently installed and registered with Python. (Note that I had to truncate the list for printing.)

```
>>> help('modules')
```

Please wait a moment while I gather a list of all available modules...

AutoComplete	_random	errno	pyexpat
AutoCompleteWindow	_sha1	faulthandler	pylab
AutoExpand	_sha256	filecmp	pyparsing
Bindings	_sha512	fileinput	pytz
CallTipWindow	_signal	fnmatch	queue

```
...
Enter any module name to get more help.  Or, type "modules
spam" to search
for modules whose name or summary contain the string "spam".
```

You can also use the help() function to get information on a specific module. First, you need to import the module. Again, the following listing was truncated for brevity.

```
>>> import math
>>> help(math)
Help on built-in module math:

NAME
    math

DESCRIPTION
    This module is always available.  It provides access to the
    mathematical functions defined by the C standard.

FUNCTIONS
    acos(...)
        acos(x)

        Return the arc cosine (measured in radians) of x.
...
FILE
    (built-in)
```

You can learn a lot more about these built-in modules on the Python documentation site at https://docs.python.org/3/py-modindex.html.

Extended Modules

In addition to the built-in modules that you get with every Python installation, there are countless extensions that you can add called packages. Fortunately, the good folks at Python have provided a method to learn about third-party packages. Visit https://pypi.python.org/pypi for more information.

Once you've found the package that you want or need to install for your application, the easiest way to install it is by using PIP. As of Python 2.7.9 and Python 3.4, the PIP binaries are included in the download. However, since the package is constantly evolving, you will likely need to upgrade it. If everything installed and configured correctly, you should be able to do this from the command line.

1.   Open a terminal window.

2.   In Windows, type

```
python -m pip install -U pip
```

3.   In Linux or macOS, type

```
pip install -U pip
```

Once that is done, you're ready to use PIP. Keep in mind that you'll run PIP from the terminal, not from within the Python shell.

For this demonstration, we'll install a package used for plotting mathematical formulas. matplotlib is a very popular package for visualizing data using Python. The actual use of this package is outside the scope of this workshop. For more information on using matplotlib, check out their website at `https://matplotlib.org`.

To install a new package, type

```
pip install matplotlib
```

This installs the matplotlib library for your use.

Custom Modules

If you have several functions that you use all the time (generally referred to as *helper functions*), you might save them in a file called myHelperFunctions.py. You can then use the `import` command to make these functions available in another program.

Generally speaking, you save your custom module file to be imported in the same file location as the program that you are working on. This is the easiest and best way to make sure that the compiler can find the file. It is possible to save the file elsewhere, but then you either include the full path for the file or make changes to the system path variables. For now, keep any module files that you create in your working directory (the same location as the program that you are working on). This helps you avoid any additional heartache.

Up until now, we've been using the IDLE shell . Let's create a custom module file, and then import that into another program.

1. Open IDLE.

2. Click **File ➤ New File**. This opens a new text editor window.

3. In the new file window, click **File ➤ Save** and name it myHelperFunctions.py.

4. Enter the following code:

```
def hello_helper():
        print("I'm helper. I help.")
```

5. Save the file.

6. Click **File ➤ New File** to create a new code file.

7. Type the following:

```
import myHelperFunctions
myHelperFunctions.hello_helper()
```

8. Save the file as hello_helper.py in the same directory that you saved myHelperFunctions.py.

9. Press F5 or select **Run ➤ Run Module** from the menu.

In the shell window, you should see this:

```
I'm helper. I help.
```

Classes

Now we get to the good stuff: classes. A class is nothing more than the logical representation of a physical or abstract entity within your code; for instance, a robot. The robot class creates a framework that describes a physical robot to the program. How you describe it is entirely up to you, but it is represented in how you build the class. This representation is abstract in much the same way the word *robot* represents the abstraction of the concept of a robot. If we were standing in a room full of robots and I said, "Hand me the robot," your response would likely be, "Which robot?" This is because the term *robot* applies to every robot in the room. But, if I were to say, "Hand me Nomad," you would know the specific robot that I was talking about. Nomad is an instance of a robot.

This is how a class is used. You start by defining the class. You do this by constructing the abstraction of the entity that you want to represent; in this case, a robot. When you want to describe a specific robot, you create an instance of the class that applies to that robot.

There is a lot to learn about classes, but the following are the key things that you need to know.

- A class is made up of functions called *methods*. Methods are functions within a class that perform work. For instance, you may have method in the robot class called `drive_forward()`. In this method, you add the code to make the robot to drive forward.

- A method always requires the `self` parameter. This parameter is a reference to the instance of the class.

- `self` is always the first parameter of a method.

- Every class must have a special method called `__init__`. The `__init__` method is called when an instance is created, and it initializes that instance of the class. In this method, you perform whatever needs to happen for the class to function. Most often, you define attributes for the class.

- The *attributes* of a class are variables within the class that describe some feature. For instance, for the robot class, we want to name some functional attributes, like direction and speed. These are created in the `__init__` method.

There are several types of methods:

- *Mutator methods*: These methods change values within the class. For instance, setters are a type of mutator method that set the value of an attribute.

- *Accessor methods*: These methods access attributes within a class.

- *Helper methods*: These include any number of methods that perform work within the class. For example, the obligatory `__init__` method is a type of helper called a *constructor*. Helper methods are anything that performs work within a class, generally for other methods; for example, a method that formats a string prior to output.

Creating a Class

Before you delve in and start writing code, I suggest you take a little time to plan what you're about to build. This doesn't need to be an extensive plan that flushes out every detail, but it is good to have at least a rough outline of what you're going to build before you build it.

Planning

The easiest way to do plan is on a sheet of paper, but if you prefer digital, your favorite text editor may do as well. You want to make a list or an outline of the class. Our example class is for a simulated wheeled robot, so we want to list the attributes that describe our robot, and then list the actions the robot will perform. These are our methods.

Initial Sample Robot Class

- Attributes
  - Name
  - Description
  - Primary color
  - Owner
- Methods
  - Drive forward
  - Drive backward
  - Turn left
  - Turn right

As you are writing your outline, imagine how you will use each method. What information, if any, will you need for it? What information, if any, will it return? If your method is expecting information in the form of parameters, is there a default value? If so, do you want to reserve the capability to change the default value programmatically? From my experience, the answer to this last question is almost always yes.

So, with these questions in mind, let's revisit the outline.

Initial Sample Robot Class

- Attributes
  - Name
  - Description
  - Primary color
  - Owner
  - Default speed (default: 125)
  - Default duration (default: 100)
- Methods
  - Drive forward (parameter: speed) (return: none)
  - Drive backward (parameter: speed) (return: none)
  - Turn left (parameter: duration) (return: none)
  - Turn right (parameter: duration) (return: none)
  - Set speed (parameter: new speed) (return: none)
  - Set duration (parameter: new duration) (return: none)

As you can see, after revisiting the outline, we added a few new attributes and a few new methods. Default speed holds an integer value between 0 and 255. Later in the book, we use this value to set the speed of our motor controller. The half speed is 125. Default duration is the amount of time the robot moves in milliseconds. The value 100 is about 1/10 of a second. We also added two methods for setting the values of these two attributes.

In most programming languages, the attributes are private, which means that they can only be accessible from code contained in the class. As such, you create get() and set() methods to view and change the values. In Python, attributes are public and can be accessed or changed with a simple `class.attribute` call. Python attributes cannot be made private; however, the tradition in Python is to prefix an attribute that you want to be private with an underscore. This indicates to other developers that the attribute should be treated as private and not modified outside a class's methods.

So, strictly speaking, the set speed and set duration methods are not strictly needed. If we want to indicate that these attributes are intended to be private and should only be updated with the method, then we precede the name with an underscore, like this:

```
_speed
_duration
```

You can create a class anywhere in your code. What makes classes so useful is that they encapsulate functionality that allows you to easily port it from one project to the next. For this reason, it is generally better to create a class as its own module and import it into your code. That is what we'll be doing here.

Let's build our robot class and then use it.

1. Create a new Python file and save it as robot_ sample_class.py.

   We'll start by declaring our class and creating the required constructor function, __init__. Right now, all we need __init__ to do is initialize the attributes and move the values from the parameters to the attributes. Note that we have declared default values for speed and duration as 125 and 100, respectively.

2. Enter the following code:

```python
class Robot():
    """

    A simple robot class
    This multi-line comment is a good place
    to provide a description of what the class
    is.
    """

    # define the initiating function.
    # speed = value between 0 and 255
    # duration = value in milliseconds
    def __init__(self, name, desc, color, owner,
                speed = 125, duration = 100):
            # initilaizes our robot
        self.name = name
        self.desc = desc
        self.color = color
        self.owner = owner
        self.speed = speed
        self.duration = duration
```

With the initialization done, let's look at writing our methods. As mentioned, methods are simply functions contained in a class that perform work within the class. Since we don't have a robot to control at the moment, we simply print confirmation messages to the shell to simulate our robot.

```python
def drive_forward(self):
        # simulates driving forward
        print(self.name.title() + " is driving" +
                " forward " + str(self.duration) +
                " milliseconds")

def drive_backward(self):
        # simulates driving backward
        print(self.name.title() + " is driving" +
                " backward " + str(self.duration) +
                " milliseconds")

def turn_left(self):
# simulates turning left
        print(self.namc.title() + " is turning " +
                " right " + str(self.duration) +
                " milliseconds")

def turn_right(self):
        # simulates turning right
        print(self.name.title() + " is turning " +
                " left " + str(self.duration) +
                " milliseconds")

def set_speed(self, speed):
        # sets the speed of the motors
        self.speed = speed
```

```
        print("the motor speed is now " +
                str(self.speed))

def set_duration(self, duration):
        # sets duration of travel
        self. duration = duration
        print("the duration is now " +
                str(self. duration))
```

3. Save the file.

   Now that we've created our new Robot class, we will use it to define Nomad as a Robot.

4. Create a new Python file and save it as `robot_sample.py`.

   We'll start by importing the `robot_sample_class` code, and then use it to create a new robot called Nomad.

5. Enter the following code:

```
import robot_sample_class
my_robot = Robot("Nomad", "Autonomous rover",
        black", "Jeff Cicolani")
```

Using the class definition to create a new instance of the class is called *instantiation*. Note that we did not provide values for the last two parameters, `speed` and `duration`. Because we provided default values for these parameters, we did not need to provide values during instantiation. If we had not provided default values, we would get an error when we tried to run the code.

With our new robot instance, let's do some work with it.

```
print("My robot is a " + my_robot.desc + " called " +
my_robot.name)

my_robot.drive_forward()
my_robot.drive_backward()
my_robot.turn_left()
my_robot.turn_right()
my_robot.set_speed(255)
my_robot.set_duration(1000)
```

6. Save the file.

7. Press F5 to run the program.

In the Python shell window, you should see something like this:

```
>>> =====================RESTART====================
>>>
My robot is an autonomous rover called Nomad
Nomad is driving forward 100 milliseconds
Nomad is driving backward 100 milliseconds
Nomad is turning left 100 milliseconds
Nomad is turning right 100 milliseconds
the motor speed is now 255
the duration is now 1000
```

Styling

Before we wrap up this chapter, I want to take a moment to talk about styling your code. We've already seen that indentation is important and must meet strict guidelines to denote code blocks and so forth. But there are a few areas where you can affect less critical styling decisions. Of course, there are traditions within the Python community that are recommended.

There are a few best practices suggested by the creators and primary developers of Python. You can read all of their suggestions in the Python Style Guide at `www.python.org/dev/peps/pep-0008/`. I recommend going through the style guide and practicing their suggestions before you develop some really bad habits (like I did). For now, let's focus on how you name your variables, functions, and classes.

Blank Lines

Leaving blank lines between code blocks for logical, visual separation is just a good idea. It makes your code easier to read.

Commenting

Write comments in your code. Do it frequently and be verbose. When you come back to read your code later (for debugging or to reuse it for another project), you will want to know what you were thinking when the code was written, and what you were trying to do with it.

If your code ever makes it out into the wild, where other people read or review it, they will need the comments, too. Python is a community, and code is shared frequently. Well-commented and described code is greatly appreciated.

Naming Conventions

How you name your variables, functions, and classes is a personal decision. Do what is most comfortable for you. Python is a case-sensitive language. Using a capital letter in one place and not another creates two different variables and endless hours of frustration.

Common variable names are not addressed in the style guide, although the convention is to use mixed-case naming. Mixed-case names start with a lowercase character, but each word in the name is capitalized; for example, `myRobots`.

Functions and modules should be lowercase. To make them easier to read, use underscores between words. So our `hello world` function is named `hello_world`.

Classes should be named using CapWords. As the name implies, CapWords capitalizes the first letter of every word, including the first character in the name. This style is more commonly known as *camel case*.

Finally, lists and other collections should be pluralized. This is an indicator that the variable represents more than one object. For instance, `robots` is a list of robots. If we were addressing an individual item in the list, it would look something like this:

```
robot = robots[0]
```

Summary

We use Python throughout this book. It is a very simple language to learn, and it provides a lot of powerful features. Many software developers think that Python is slow. But where it is slow in some areas, it more than makes up time in other areas, as you will see when we start working with computer vision in Chapter 9.

CHAPTER 4

Raspberry Pi GPIO

Previous chapters introduced the Raspberry Pi hardware, and you learned how to use Python to program it. You installed the operating system, configured it for your use, and set up remote access so that you can program the Pi without connecting a keyboard, mouse, and monitor directly to it. You learned the basic structure of a Python program, syntax, and enough about the language to start writing programs.

Next, you are going to learn how to use the Raspberry Pi's GPIO interface to interact with the physical world. This is crucial for robotics because it's how the processor detects what is happening around it and responds to outside stimuli. Without the capability to detect and act on the physical world, any kind of intelligent autonomy is not possible.

Raspberry Pi GPIO

There are several ways to connect to the Raspberry Pi. By far the simplest is through one of the USB ports built into the board. The USB ports provide four serial connections through which you can access outside components, such as the keyboard and mouse we used to set up the Pi. However, the USB port requires special hardware to convert the serial commands to the signals needed to operate the device. The Raspberry Pi has a more direct method of connecting to external devices: the GPIO header.

© Jeff Cicolani 2018
J. Cicolani, *Beginning Robotics with Raspberry Pi and Arduino*,
https://doi.org/10.1007/978-1-4842-3462-4_4

GPIO is the interface between the electronics and the rest of the world. A *header* generally refers to a set of pins on a board that allows access to certain functionalities. The GPIO header is the pair of 20-pin rows running along one edge of the board (see Figure 4-1), which is referred to as a 40-pin header.

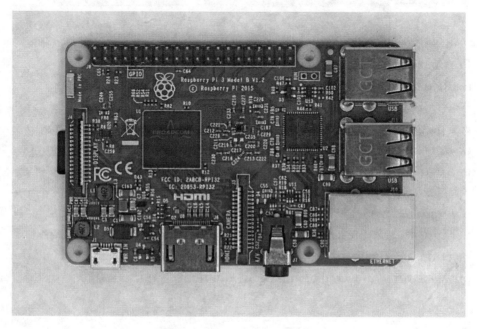

Figure 4-1. *Raspberry Pi with 40-pin header*

It is very important to note that the header provides a direct connection to the electronics on the board. There is neither a buffer nor safety features built into these pins. This means that if you connect something incorrectly or use the wrong voltage, you will likely damage your Pi. The following are things that you need to be aware of before working with the header:

- Although the Raspberry Pi is powered with a 5-volt USB micro adapter, the electronics are 3.3 volts. This means that you need to pay attention to the voltages that the sensors use.

- There are two voltages supplied on the GPIO pins: 5V and 3.3V. Be careful which one you are using, especially if attempting to power the Pi through GPIO.

- It is possible to power the Raspberry Pi through one of the 5V GPIO pins; however, circuit protection and regulation is not provided. If you supply too much voltage, or there is a current spike, the board may be damaged. If you must use the GPIO pins to power the board, be sure to provide an external regulator.

- There are two numbering schemas for the GPIO header: board and BCM. This means that there are two different ways to reference the pins from your code; the one that you decide to use is generally up to you. You just have to remember which schema you chose to go with.

Pin Numbering

As I mentioned, there are two numbering schemas for the 40-pin header: board and BCM.

Board numbering simply numbers the pins sequentially. Pin 1 is the one closest to the micro SD card, and pin 2 is the adjacent pin closest to the outer edge of the Pi. The numbering continues this way, with odd-numbered pins on the inside row and even-numbered pins on the outside. Pin 40 is the pin on the edge of the board, near the USB ports.

BCM numbering is not nearly as straightforward. BCM stands for Broadcom, the manufacturer of the SoC (system on a chip) that drives the Pi. On the Raspberry Pi 2, the processor is the BCM2836; on the Raspberry Pi 3, it's the BCM2837. BCM numbering refers to the pin numbers of the Broadcom chip, which can vary between versions. The BCM2836 and BCM2837 have the same pin-out, so there is no difference between the Pi 2 and Pi 3.

To make connecting electronic components to the 40-pin header, we will use the Adafruit T-Cobbler Plus and a breadboard. The T-Cobbler has pin information stenciled on the board for quick reference; however, the T-Cobbler uses BCM numbering. Thus, we will use BCM numbering.

Connecting to the Raspberry Pi

There are several ways to connect the pins from the header to other devices. The motor controller that we will use is an example of a board that sits directly on top of the header. In Raspberry Pi terminology, these boards are referred to as *hats* or *plates*.

Another option is to directly connect to the pins using jumpers. For many people, this is the preferred method during prototyping.

I prefer a third method, which is to use another board from Adafruit called the Pi Cobbler. There are a few versions of the cobbler, but I prefer the Adafruit T-Cobbler Plus for Raspberry Pi (see Figure 4-2). This board is designed to attach to a breadboard via a ribbon cable. It uses a 40-pin header configured perpendicular to the pins that plug into the breadboard. This moves the ribbon cable attachment off the breadboard and allows better access to the holes.

Figure 4-2. *T-Cobbler mounted on the breadboard*

One advantage of using the cobbler is that the pin breakouts are clearly marked. When we start building our circuits, it will be very easy to see exactly what you are hooking up. This also makes it easier to identify which pins are being used for your code. When you declare pin 21 as an output pin, you will know exactly which pin it is on the board.

Limitations of Raspberry Pi's GPIO

There are a few things to keep in mind as you are working with GPIO.

First, the Raspberry Pi that we set up is not a real-time device. Debian Linux is a full operating system with many layers of abstraction from the hardware. This means that commands to the hardware are not direct. Rather, the commands are passed through several operations before and after the CPU sends them to the board. Python operates in another abstraction layer. Each of these layers introduces a certain degree of lag.

It's generally not perceivable to us, but it can make a huge difference in robot operations. There are distributions of Debian that are more real time, designed for industrial applications, but the standard Raspbian version that we are using is not one of these.

Second, there is no analog input on the Pi. Well, there is one, but it is shared with the serial port, which we will likely use later for something else. So, it's better to accept that there are no analog input pins. You will see why this is important in Chapter 5.

Third, the Pi only has two PWM capable pins. PWM stands for *pulse width modulation*, which is how we send a varied signal to an external device. This means that there are only two pins on the header that can simulate an analog output. Both of these pins are also shared with the audio output of the Pi, which is not optimal.

The good news is there's a simple solution for all of these issues, which is simply to introduce an external microcontroller that is in real time, offers multiple analog inputs, and provides more than two PWM outputs. We will use this with the Arduino in Chapter 5. The Arduino is basically a prototyping board for the AVR AT series of microcontrollers. These chips are directly connected to the hardware and do not have the layers of abstraction that you find in most SoC processors, like those on the Pi. There are other advantages to using an Arduino, which I discuss in Chapter 5.

Accessing GPIO with Python

Hardware is only part of the equation. We'll use our new Python skills to program the behavior we want. In order to do that, we'll use the RPi.GPIO library. You will recall from Chapter 3 that a library is a collection of classes and functions that provide additional functionality.

In robotics, a new piece of hardware, sensor, or other component frequently has a library to allow you to use it more easily. Sometimes the library is generic, such as RPi.GPIO; other times, the library is made for a specific device. For example, we will use a library specific to the motor controller board in Chapter 7. As you add more hardware to your robot, you frequently have to download the new libraries from the manufacturer's website. You will see this in action when we start working with the motor controller.

The GPIO library provides objects and functions to access the GPIO pins. Raspbian comes with the library installed, so it should be ready to go. For more information on how to use the package, visit `https://sourceforge.net/p/raspberry-gpio-python/wiki/BasicUsage/`.

To use the GPIO library, we need to do two things: import the package and then tell it which mode we'll use to access the pins. As I discussed earlier, there are two modes—board and BCM—that essentially tell the system which numbering reference to use.

Board mode references the numbering on the P1 header of the Raspberry Pi. Since this numbering remains constant, for backward compatibility, you won't need to change your pin numbering in your code, based on the board revision.

In contrast, BCM mode refers to the pin numbering from the Broadcom SoC, which means that on newer versions of the Pi, it is possible for the pin layout to change. Fortunately, this pin layout has not changed between the BCM2836 used in the Pi 2, and the BCM2837 used in the Pi3.

For our purposes, we'll use BCM mode—simply because that is what is illustrated on the T-Cobbler.

Every program using the GPIO header includes the following two lines of code:

```
import RPi.GPIO as GPIO
GPIO.setmode(GPIO.BCM)
```

Simple Output: LED Example

The simplest example is the ubiquitous hardware version of "Hello World"—the blinking LED. Our first GPIO project is to connect an LED to the Pi and to use a Python script to make the LED blink. Let's start by hooking up the circuit. To do this, you need a breadboard, the T-Cobbler, an LED, a 220ohm (Ω) resistor, and two short pieces of wire to use as jumpers.

Hooking Up the Circuit

1. Attach the T-Cobbler as shown in Figure 4-3. One row of pins should be on either side of the split in the board. The placement is up to you; however, I generally attach it such that the ribbon cable header is off the board. This allows maximum access to the breadboard.

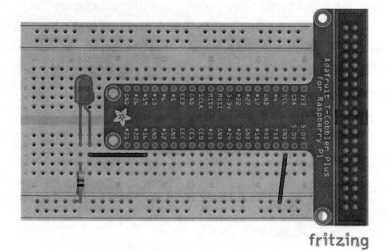

Figure 4-3. *Circuit layout for the LED example*

2. Connect the 220Ω resistor between the ground rail and an empty 5-hole rail.

3. Connect the LED cathode to the same rail as the resistor. The cathode is the pin closest to the flat side of the LED. On some LEDs, this pin is shorter than the other pin (see Figure 4-4).

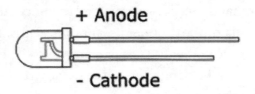

Figure 4-4. *LED polarity*

4. Connect the LED anode to another empty 5-pin rail.

5. Connect a jumper from the anode's rail to the rail connected to pin 16 on the T-Cobbler.

6. Connect a jumper from the ground rail that the LED is connected to and a rail connected to any of the ground pins of the T-Cobbler.

If you want to test the LED before moving on to the code, you can move the jumper from pin 16 to one of the 3.3V pins. If your Pi is powered on, the LED will illuminate. Make sure that you move the jumper back to pin 16 before continuing.

Writing the Code

The code for this project is very simple. It is written in Python 3. Although the code works in either version, one of the lines will not work in Python 2.7. Specifically, the print line at the end uses the end parameter, which is not compatible. If you are using Python 2.7, you will need to omit this parameter.

The end parameter replaces the default /n that is appended to each printed line, with a /r. The /r is a carriage return as opposed to the new line represented by /n. This means that the cursor returns to the beginning of the current line, and any new text overwrites the pervious characters. It does not clear the line first, however. So we append an arbitrary number of empty spaces to the end of the new text to ensure that all the previous text is completely removed.

The GPIO commands access system–level memory. All system-level commands must run with super user or root access. This means that you need to run Python with sudo or grant yourself permanent root permissions, which can be dangerous. Once we've written the code, we will execute in from the command. We have to make the file executable before we do this, but that is simple to do from the terminal.

To start, let's create a new Python 3 file by using IDLE or on the terminal. If using IDLE, do the following:

1. Open IDLE for Python 3.

2. Click **New**.

3. Save the file as gpio_led.py in your project folder.

If using a terminal, do the following:

1. Open the terminal window.

2. Navigate to your project folder. On my Pi, it is
   $ cd ~/TRG-RasPi-Robot/code

3. Type **touch gpio_led.py**.

4. Type **idle3 gpio_led.py**.

   This opens the empty file in the IDLE IDE for Python 3.

5. Once your file is created and you are in the IDLE
    editor, enter the following code:

```
# GPIO example blinking LED

# Import the GPIO and time libraries
import RPi.GPIO as GPIO
import time

# Set the GPIO mode to BCM and disable warnings
GPIO.setmode(GPIO.BCM)
GPIO.setwarnings(False)

# Define pins
led = 16

GPIO.setup(led,GPIO.OUT)

# Make sure LED is off
GPIO.output(led,False)

# Begin Loop
while True:

    # Turn LED on
    GPIO.output(led,True)

    # Wait 1 second
    time.sleep(1)

    # Turn LED off
    GPIO.output(led,False)

    # Wait 1 second
    time.sleep(1)
```

6. Save the file.

Next, we will use the terminal to make the file executable and then run it.

1. Open a new terminal window and navigate to your project folder.

2. Type **chmod +x gpio_led.py**.

    This makes the file executable.

3. To run the code, type **sudo python3 gpio_led.py**.

There you have it: a blinking LED. Hello world.

Pulse Width Modulation (PWM)

Even though there are only two PWM pins on the Pi's GPIO header, and you likely won't use them, it is useful to know how to control them properly. The two PWM pins on the board are 18 and 19. For this example, we'll set up the LED to use pin 18 and pulse the LED.

Hooking Up the Circuit

All right, this is the complicated part. To set up this circuit, you need to follow these directions very closely. Use the circuit we built for the LED exercise.

1. Move the jumper from pin 16 to pin 18.

Phew. Now that we've gotten through all of that, let's code.

Writing the Code

Create a new Python 3 file.

If using IDLE, do the following:

1. Open IDLE for Python 3.

2. Click **New**.

3. Save the file as gpio_pwm_led.py in your project folder.

If using a terminal, do the following:

1. In the terminal window, navigate to your project folder. On my Pi, it is

   ```
   $ cd ~/TRG-RasPi-Robot/code.
   ```

2. Type **touch gpio_pwm_led.py**.

3. Type **idle3 gpio_pwm_led.py**.

   This opens the empty file in the IDLE IDE for Python 3.

4. Once your file is created and you are in the IDLE editor, enter the following code:

```
# GPIO example blinking LED

# Import the GPIO and time libraries
import RPi.GPIO as GPIO
import time

# Set the GPIO mode to BCM and disable warnings
GPIO.setmode(GPIO.BCM)
GPIO.setwarnings(False)

# Define pins
pwmPin = 18

GPIO.setup(pwmPin,GPIO.OUT)
pwm = GPIO.PWM(pwmPin,100)

# Make sure LED is off
pwm.start(0)

# Begin Loop
while True:
```

```
count = 1
# begin while loop to brighten LED
while count < 100:

    # set duty cycle
    pwm.ChangeDutyCycle(count)

    # delay 1/100 of a second
    time.sleep(0.01)

    # increment count
    count = count + 1

# begin while loop to dim LED
while count > 1:

    pwm.ChangeDutyCycle(count)

    time.sleep(0.01)

    # set duty cycle
    pwm.ChangeDutyCycle(count)

    # delay 1/100 of a second
    time.sleep(0.01)

    # decrement count
    count = count - 1
```

5. Open a new terminal window and navigate to your project folder.

6. Type **chmod +x gpio_pwm_led.py** to make the file executable.

7. To run the code, type

    sudo python3 gpio_pwm_led.py

Your LED should now be pulsing. To change the rate at which it pulses, change the value in the `time.sleep()` function calls.

Simple Input

Now that we've seen how easy it is to send out a signal, it's time to get some information back into the Pi. We'll do this through two examples. First, the push-button; in this example, the Pi is set up to take input from a simple push-button and indicate in the terminal when the button has been pushed. The second example uses a sonic rangefinder to read the distance to an object. The output will be displayed in the terminal.

Push-button Example

The simplest form of input is a push-button. You press a button, the circuit closes, and something happens. For our first input example, we will connect a push-button to the GPIO header.

There are essentially two ways to connect a push-button. You can set it up to start in a low state, which means that when the button is not pushed, there is no signal going to the pin, and the voltage on the pin is read as "low" by the processor. You can also connect it in a high state. In this configuration, the pin reads as high, or on, when the button is not pushed. When the button is pushed, the pin is brought to the low state.

You frequently hear the terms *pulling high* or *pulling low*. Pulling a pin high or low is the method that forces the pin into a high or a low state. In many applications, this is done by adding a resistor to the circuit.

A resistor connected between the logic pin and the voltage causes the pin to be in a high state. The pin is *pulled high*. The button is then connected to ground. When the button is pushed, the voltage flows through the button to ground, bypassing the pin. With no voltage going to the pin, it goes into a low state.

Conversely, connecting the resistor between the logic pin and ground, and then connecting the button between the pin and the voltage source, the pin is pulled down. While the button is open, any residual voltage in the pin is drawn to ground, leaving the pin in a low state. When the button is pushed, voltage is applied to the pin and it goes into a high state.

Pins are pulled high or low to assure that they are in the expected state when the button is pushed. It's a way to explicitly tell the circuit how it is expected to behave, and it's generally a good practice.

Fortunately, the Raspberry Pi has built-in circuitry to accommodate pulling a pin high or low. This means that we can pull a pin to the proper state through code, and we don't have to worry about adding extra components.

For this exercise, let's pull the pin high. When the button is pushed, the pin goes low and a message prints to the terminal window.

Hooking up the Circuit

The following parts are needed for this exercise:

- Tactile push-button switch

- 4 male-to-male jumpers

1. Attach the T-Cobbler as shown in Figure 4-5. One row of pins should be on either side of the split in the board. The placement is up to you; however, I generally attach it so that the ribbon cable header is off the board. This allows maximum access to the breadboard.

Figure 4-5. *Push-button example circuit layout*

2. Connect a tactile push-button so that the pins bridge the gap in the center of the breadboard.

3. Connect a jumper between the 3.3V pin and the voltage rail.

4. Connect another jumper between the ground pin and the ground rail.

5. Use another jumper to connect one side of the tactile switch to the ground rail.

6. Use the remaining jumper to connect the other button pin to pin 17.

These tactile switches are double pole, single throw (DPST). This means that when the button is pushed, the two pins on one side of the breadboard gap are connected. The pins on the other side of the gap form a separate circuit. Be sure that the jumpers are going to pins on the same side of the divide.

Writing the Code

Create a new Python 3 file.

If using IDLE, do the following:

1. Open IDLE for Python 3.

2. Click **New**.

3. Save the file as gpio_button.py in your project folder.

If using a terminal window, do the following:

1. Navigate to your project folder. On my Pi it is

   $ cd ~/TRG-RasPi-Robot/code.

2. Type **touch gpio_button.py**.

3. Type **idle3 gpio_button.py**. This opens the empty file in the IDLE IDE for Python 3.

4. Enter the following code:

```
# GPIO example using an NC-SR04 ultrasonic rangefinder

# import the GPIO and time libraries
import RPi.GPIO as GPIO

# Set the GPIO mode to BCM mode and disable warnings
GPIO.setmode(GPIO.BCM)
GPIO.setwarnings(False)

# Define pin
btnPin = 20
GPIO.setup(btnPin, GPIO.IN, pull_up_down = GPIO.PUD_UP)
```

```
# Begin while loop
while True:
        btnVal = GPIO.input(btnPin)

        # If the pin is low, print to terminal
        if (btnVal == false):
                print('Button pressed')
```

5. Open a new terminal window and navigate to your project folder.

6. Type **chmod +x gpio_button.py**.

7. To run the code, type **sudo python3 gpio_button.py**

Sonic Rangefinder Example

For this example, let's use the HC-SR04 ultrasonic sensor to determine the distance to an object. You'll put the call into a loop that allows us to get constant distance readings. You'll use the libraries used in the previous example to access the GPIO pins.

This exercise introduces you to one of the key factors to watch out for with the Pi and many other devices: voltage difference between the sensors and the pins. Many sensors are designed to work at 5 volts. The Pi, however, uses 3.3 volts in its logic. That means all of the I/O pins are designed to work with 3.3 volts. Applying a 5V signal to any of these pins can cause severe damage to your Pi. The Pi does provide a few 5V source pins, but we need to reduce the returning signal to 3.3 volts.

Hooking Up the Circuit

This time, the circuit is a bit more complicated. Really. Keep in mind that the sensor works on 5 volts. The Pi's GPIO pins work on 3.3 volts. Feeding a 5V return signal into a 3.3V pin can damage the Pi. To keep that from happening, let's add a simple voltage divider to the echo pin.

Let's do some math.

$$V_{out} = V_{in} * \frac{R1}{R1+R2}$$

$$V_{out} = V_{in} * \frac{R2}{R2+R1}$$

$$\frac{V_{out}}{V_{in}} = \frac{R2}{R1+R2}$$

We have 5 volts in and want 3.3 volts out, and we are using a 1kΩ resistor as part of the circuit. So...

$$\frac{3.3}{5} = \frac{R2}{1000+R2}$$

$$0.66 = \frac{R2}{1000+R2}$$

$$0.66(1000+R2) = R2$$

$$660 + 0.66R2 = R2$$

$$660 + 0.34R2$$

$$1941 = R2$$

The following is the parts list:

- HC-SR04

- 1kΩ resistor

- 2kΩ resistor

  You can use two 1kΩ resistors in series, or a more popular, similar resistor is the 2.2kΩ. That's what we'll use.

- 4 male-to-female jumpers

- 4 male-to-male jumpers

Here's the setup.

1. Attach the T-Cobbler, as shown in Figure 4-6. One row of pins should be on either side of the split in the board. The placement is up to you; however, I generally attach it so that the ribbon cable header is off the board. This allows maximum access to the breadboard.

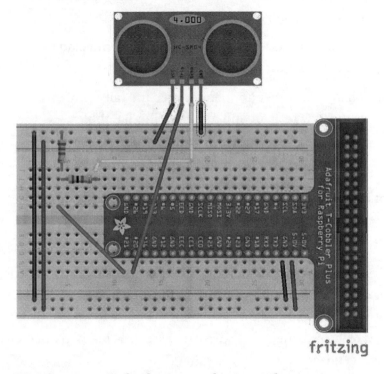

Figure 4-6. Sonic rangefinder example circuit layout

2. Make sure that the ground jumper is secure between the ground pin and the ground rail.

3. Add a jumper between one of the 5V pins and the power rail.

4. Use a male-to-female jumper to connect the ground pin on the SR04 to the ground rail.

5. Connect the VCC or 5V pin from the SR04 to the power rail.

6. Connect the trig pin on the SR04 to pin 20 of the T-Cobbler.

7. Connect the 2kΩ resistor from an empty 5-pin rail to the ground rail.

8. Connect the 1kΩ resistor from the rail connected to the 2kΩ resistor to another empty 5-pin rail.

9. Connect another jumper between the rail connected to the 2kΩ resistor and pin 21 on the T-Cobbler.

10. Connect the SR04 echo pin to the rail that the other end of the 1kΩ resistor is connected to.

That completes the wiring. Now let's get the code set up.

Writing the Code

The HC-SR04 ultrasonic rangefinder works by measuring the time it takes for an ultrasonic pulse to return to the sensor. We'll send out a 10-microsecond pulse and then listen for the pulse to return. By measuring the length of the returned pulse, we can use a little math to calculate the distance in centimeters.

Distance is calculated as speed × time. It's derived from the formula speed = distance ÷ time. At sea level, sound travels at a rate of 343m per second, or 34,300cm per second. Since we are actually measuring the time it takes for the pulse to reach its target and return, we really only need half of that value. Let's working with the following formula:

$$Distance = 17,150 \times time$$

The code simply sends out a 10µS pulse, measures the time it takes to return, calculates the estimated distance in centimeters, and displays it in the terminal window.

Create a new Python 3 file.

If using IDLE, do the following:

1.   Open IDLE for Python 3.

2.   Click **New**.

3.   Save the file as gpio_sr04.py in your project folder.

If using a terminal window, do the following:

1.   Navigate to your project folder. On my Pi it is

      $ cd ~/TRG-RasPi-Robot/code

2.   Type **touch gpio_sr04.py**.

3.   Type **idle3 gpio_sr04.py**. This opens the empty file in the IDLE IDE for Python 3.

4.   Enter the following code:

```
# GPIO example using an NC-SR04 ultrasonic rangefinder

# import the GPIO and time libraries
import RPi.GPIO as GPIO
import time

# Set the GPIO mode to BCM mode and disable warnings
GPIO.setmode(GPIO.BCM)
GPIO.setwarnings(False)

# Define pins
trig = 20
echo = 21
```

```
GPIO.setup(trig,GPIO.OUT)
GPIO.setup(echo,GPIO.IN)

print("Measuring distance")

# Begin while loop
while True:
    # Set trigger pin low got 1/10 second
    GPIO.output(trig,False)
    time.sleep(0.1)

    # Send a 10uS pulse
    GPIO.output(trig,True)
    time.sleep(0.00001)
    GPIO.output(trig,False)

    # Get the start and end times of the return pulse
    while GPIO.input(echo)==0:
        pulse_start = time.time()

    while GPIO.input(echo)==1:
        pulse_end = time.time()

    pulse_duration = pulse_end - pulse_start

    # Calculate the distance in centimeters
    distance = pulse_duration * 17150
    distance = round(distance, 2)

    # Display the results. end = '\r' forces the output to the
    same line
    print("Distance: " + str(distance) + "cm        ", end = '\r')
```

5. Open a new terminal window and navigate to your project folder.

6. Type `chmod +x gpio_sr04.py`.

7. To run the code, type **sudo python3 gpio_sr04.py**

Summary

One of the great things about the Raspberry Pi is the GPIO header. The 40-pin header allows you to interface directly with sensors and other devices. In addition to the simple GPIO we used to connect to the LED, button, and ultrasonic sensor, there are pins with other specific functions. I suggest exploring some of these other functions. Pins marked SCL, SDA, MISO, and MOSI are serial connections that allow you to use advanced sensors, such as accelerometers and GPS.

When working with the GPIO header, there are a few things that you need to keep in mind.

- To run your script, first make the file executable by using `chmod +x <filename>`.

- Whenever you are running scripts that use the GPIO pins, you need to use `sudo`.

- Pay careful attention to the voltages used by your sensors.

- Although the header can supply 5 volts for devices, the logic pins are 3.3 volts. You will damage your Raspberry Pi if you don't reduce the signal coming from the sensor.

- A voltage splitting circuit—like the one built for the ultrasonic sensor—can be used to reduce 5V signals from sensors to 3.3 volts.

- Premade boards called logic level shifters reduce the voltage.

- The Raspberry Pi has no functionally useful analog pins.

- It has only two PWM channels. Each of these is connected to two pins, so it may look like it has four usable PWM pins, but it really doesn't.

In the next chapter, we connect an Arduino board to our Raspberry Pi. The Arduino is a microcontroller designed for IO. That is all it does, but it does it well. By combining these two boards, we not only overcome the Pi's shortcomings, but also add other benefits.

CHAPTER 5

Raspberry Pi and Arduino

In Chapter 4, we used the GPIO pins on the Raspberry Pi to interact with an LED and an ultrasonic sensor. Many times, this is enough to do what you want to do. However, I also discussed some of the shortcomings of the Raspberry Pi GPIO and the likely need to expand the capabilities of the Pi in order to overcome these shortcomings.

In this chapter, we introduce a microcontroller to our robot. A microcontroller is a device, usually in chip form, designed to work directly with other components through input and output pins. Each pin is attached to the microcontroller's circuitry and serves a specific purpose.

Because the pins are directly attached to the microcontroller's sensitive inner workings, additional circuitry is generally needed to make it safe to work with it. Many manufacturers provide an evaluation board to allow developers to build prototype and proof-of-concept devices quickly.

One such board was actually developed by developers, rather than the chip manufacturer, and made available to the public. Due to its ease of use, ample documentation, and superb community support, this device quickly became a favorite of the hobby community. I am talking about the Arduino, of course.

© Jeff Cicolani 2018
J. Cicolani, *Beginning Robotics with Raspberry Pi and Arduino*,
https://doi.org/10.1007/978-1-4842-3462-4_5

We cover a lot of information about the Arduino: how to install the software, write programs (called *sketches*), and load those programs to the Arduino board. We also cover how to get your Raspberry Pi and Arduino boards to talk to each other. This adds exponentially more capabilities to your robot.

But before we go into the Arduino, let's review some of the shortcomings of the Raspberry Pi.

Raspberry Pi's GPIO in Review

In particular, let's talk about the lack of sufficient analog and pulse width modulation (PWM) pins.

Real-Time or Near Real-Time Processing

Real time processing is the system's ability to interact directly with GPIO and external devices. It is crucial for CNC applications or other applications where immediate response is required. In robotics terms, it is necessary for closed loop systems where an immediate response to stimuli is required.

A good example is an edge detector for a mobile robot. You want the robot to stop moving before it drives itself over a cliff or off the edge of a table. Taking the time it takes to process through the many abstraction layers of an operating system to reach the logic to determine to stop and then send the signal through the many layers to the motor controller could prove catastrophic. And, if the OS delays the operation or hangs, the robot will happily plummet to its demise, never the wiser. Instead, you want your robot to stop immediately.

Although there are flavors of Linux that facilitate near-real-time processing, these are specialty operating systems and the Raspbian installation we are using is not one of them.

Analog Input

We have seen digital input working on the Pi. In fact, we used the ultrasonic rangefinder to detect range when a digital pin turned on and then off (went high, then low). With a little math, we were able to convert that signal into useful data. That was a digital signal; it simply detected when a pin had a high voltage, and then when the same pin had a low voltage.

There are a many types of analog signals; not just high or low, white or black, or on or off, but also a range of values—or shades of gray to use the black/white analogy. This is very useful when you are using a sensor that measures intensity or the level of something. A light sensor that uses a photoresistor is one example. As the light intensity changes, so does the resistance, and therefore the voltage, on the sensor. A device called an *analog-to-digital converter* (ADC) transforms that analog signal into a digital value the program can use.

The Raspberry Pi has a single analog pin. This is not very useful, especially when it's tied to another function that the board likely uses—in this case, serial communication. If we were to dedicate the pin to analog input, we would not be able to use that serial channel. Even if we weren't planning to use that particular serial channel, a single analog input has very limited use.

Analog Output

Analog output is similar, in nature, to analog input. With the LED exercise we did earlier, we used a digital signal to turn an LED on and off. Analog allows us to change the brightness, or intensity of the LED. However, a digital system, such as a computer or microprocessor, cannot create a true analog signal.

It adjusts the frequency and duration of the digital signal. The duration of a digital signal is referred to as a *pulse*. Adjusting how often a pulse is active in a given time period, and the length of that pulse, is called *pulse-width modulation*, or PWM. When we were measuring the signal from the ultrasonic rangefinder, we were actually measuring the pulse returned from the device.

The Raspberry Pi has four PWM pins available. However, those four pins are connected to only two PWM processes. So, this means we only have two PWM channels available for use. And again, this is not as useful as we would like. With a real-time processor, we could simulate PWM with software. However, as discussed earlier, the Raspberry Pi is not a real-time system. So, we need to find another solution if we want more than two PWM channels.

Arduino to the Rescue

Fortunately, there is a class of device designed, specifically, to manage input and output of various types, in real time. These are microprocessors. There are many types of microprocessors out there. Some of the more common, and easy to use, are the AVR ATTiny and the ATMega processors.

However, these are chips, and unless you're used to working with them, they can be difficult to access and use. To make these devices easier to use, the manufacturers create what are known as *development boards*. These boards connect the pins on the chip to headers that are easier to access for prototyping. They also add the electronics needed to use the pins, such as voltage regulators, pull up resistors, filter caps, diodes, and so forth. So, in the end, all you have to do is connect your specific electronics to the device and prototype your product.

A few years back, a group of engineers in Italy got together and did something a little unprecedented. They developed their own development board around the AVR ATMega chip, made the design open to the public (open hardware), and then marketed it to hobbyists and students. They called this board *Arduino*. Figure 5-1 shows a typical Arduino Uno. I'm sure that it had the intended consequence of becoming a de facto standard in the hobby and maker community.

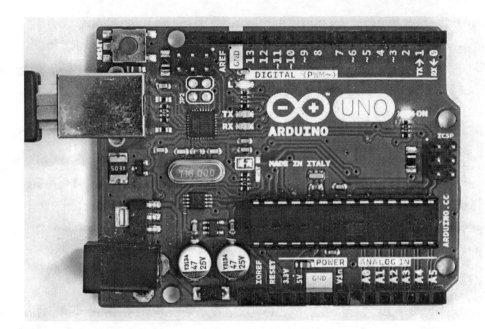

Figure 5-1. *Arduino Uno*

We will use an Arduino Uno with our Raspberry Pi. Why? First, it is a real-time processor. The Arduino communicates directly with the pins and attached peripherals. There is no lag due to OS or program layer abstraction. Second, it provides a lot more pins to work with. Among them are six analog pins and six hardware-based PWM pins that we add. It's "hardware based" because the board is real-time and we can simulate PWM signals (through software) on any of the pins (there are 20, by the way).

And that is just the Arduino Uno. There is a larger version of the Arduino board called the Mega. The Mega has 54 digital pins and 16 analog pins. That is a total of 70 pins of IO goodness.

Arduino is open hardware, which means that the designs are available for anyone to build them. As such, you find many different versions from many different manufacturers at many price points. This is a prime example of you get what you pay for. If you're just getting started, I recommend spending a little more to get a more reliable board. Later, as you develop a better understanding, and a higher tolerance for troubleshooting, you can experiment with the less expensive boards.

Using Arduino

Arduino is remarkably easy to program and use. Many people get intimidated by the prospect of working with electronics and programming hardware. But, there's a reason why so many people get their start in robotics and IoT with Arduino. Connecting devices to the Arduino is very easy, especially with the use of add-ons called *shields*.

Programming the Arduino is also very easy. Arduino provides an interface for programming the board called, simply enough, Arduino. Or more accurately, it is the Arduino IDE (integrated development environment). The Arduino IDE uses a flavor of C programming also called Arduino. As you can see, the hardware, software, and development environment are conceptually the same thing. When you talk about programming Arduino there is no distinction between the software and hardware since the only purpose of the software is to interact with the hardware.

Throughout this chapter, you need to have the Arduino IDE installed and an Arduino connected to your computer. It's assumed that the installation instructions and exercises are run on your Raspberry Pi, but in all honesty, the installation on another machine is just as easy. So, if you are more comfortable working on something other than the Pi, or you simply don't feel like remoting into one, you can do all the exercises on your PC or laptop.

Installing the Arduino IDE

Before we connect the Arduino to our Raspberry Pi, we'll want to install the software and drivers. Fortunately, this is super easy. Installing the Arduino IDE also installs any drivers that are needed to work with the Pi.

Installing the Arduino IDE

1. Open a terminal window.

2. Type **sudo apt-get install Arduino**.

3. Answer yes to any prompts.

4. Grab a drink. This may take a surprisingly long time.

When the installation process is done, it adds the Arduino IDE to your programming menu.

Connecting an Arduino

When I originally outlined this portion of the book, my intent was to provide multiple ways to connect the Arduino to the Raspberry Pi. However, to use anything but the USB port introduces another layer of complexity and Linux detail that is beyond the scope of this introduction. It essentially involves telling the Pi that you are activating the UART pins, and then disabling a number of native functions that use this channel. This is an unnecessary process to go through, especially since there are four USB ports ready to go, and if you need more you can always add a USB hub. So, we'll use a USB connection so that we can focus on the introduction to Arduino as it relates to the Pi.

To connect the Arduino, all we have to do is connect the USB cable from the Raspberry Pi to the Arduino, as depicted in Figure 5-2. Depending on the manufacturer of the board, you may need a different USB cable. Since I am using an original Uno, I use a USB A-to-B cable. Some people use a USB mini cable, and others use a USB micro.

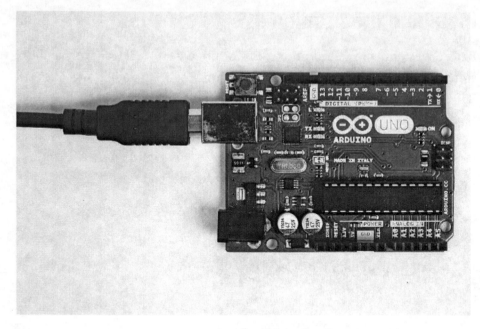

Figure 5-2.   *USB A to B cable connected to the Arduino Uno*

That's it. Since the Arduino board is powered by your Pi through the USB cable, you don't need to add external power. You're just about ready to start using your Arduino. Next, we're going to test your Arduino with the ubiquitous blink program. But first, let's look at the interface.

Programming Arduino

As I've said before, programming the Arduino is very easy. However, since we just spent a lot of time learning Python, it's very important to understand some of the differences.

We'll start by looking at the interface and some of the tricks to using it. Then we'll write a small program to illustrate the anatomy and syntax of the language. All of this is to prepare you for the next section, where we take a deeper look at the Arduino programming language.

The Arduino IDE

When first you open the Arduino IDE, you are presented with a remarkably simple interface (see Figure 5-3). The developers adopted the interface of the Programming language and IDE when they developed Arduino. If you have done any coding in the past, this interface is going to seem lacking in features. That is both purposeful and a bit misleading.

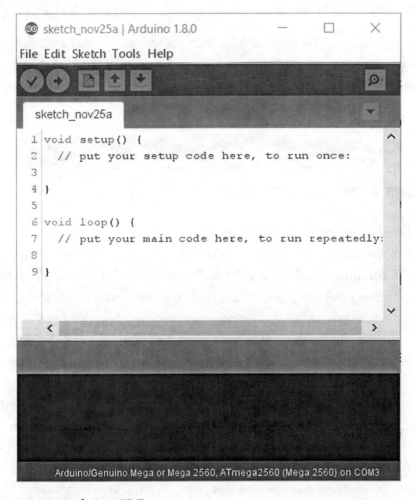

Figure 5-3. *Arduino IDE*

Despite the simple interface, the IDE is surprisingly robust. Most importantly, it provides the cross-compiling needed to get your code, written on a Linux, Windows, or Apple machine, to work on the much simpler AVC processor.

Let's walk through some of the key features and operations in the Arduino IDE.

Icons and the Menu

Being Arduino and different, the icons in the toolbar at the top of the interface are not what you're likely used to. Looking at Figure 5-4 and moving from left to right, the icons are compile, upload, new sketch, open, save, and way over to the right is the serial monitor.

Figure 5-4. *Arduino IDE toolbar*

The first two icons are very important.

Compile tells the IDE to process your code and gets it ready to load onto the Arduino board. It runs through your code and tries to build the final machine level program. At this time, it identifies any errors that you may have entered. Arduino does not provide any debugging functionality, so you depend on the compiling function quite a bit.

Upload compiles the sketch and then upload it to the board. Because the upload function runs the compiler first, you get the same compilation activities as the compile function, but, at the end of the process, it attempts to load the compiled code to your board. Since the AVR processor can only store and run one program at a time, every time that you upload to the Arduino board, you overwrite whatever is currently on there. This is not always desirable. Sometimes you compile code intermittently to check syntax and to make sure that it's right. You won't always want to load these intermediary steps to the board.

However, in the end, you need to upload your sketch to see anything happen. Compiling the sketch assures that you have working code. Whether or not the code is doing what you want it to do is another story. You won't know this until it's uploaded.

Creating a New Sketch

You can create a new sketch by either clicking the New Sketch icon in the toolbar or by clicking File ➤ New from the menu. Creating a new sketch always opens a new instance of the IDE. Whatever you were working on in the previous window is still there.

The first time you open the Arduino IDE, you are presented with the framework of a new sketch. This is also what you see when you create one later. Every Arduino sketch contains these elements. The New Sketch operation always prepopulates the IDE with this framework. You'll see what these elements are when we write our first sketch.

Saving a Sketch

Before you can compile or run a sketch, you need to save it. You can save a sketch at any time, it just must be done before you can compile or upload it. To save a sketch, click the Save icon or select File ➤ Save from the menu.

When a sketch is first saved, the system automatically creates a project folder for it. This is where the code file (with the .ino extension) is saved. Any other files created for the project are also saved in this folder. This is important when you work with larger, more complex programs, or when you start breaking your sketches up into different tabs in the IDE.

Opening Exiting Sketches

By default, when you open the IDE, the last sketch you were working on opens automatically. This is convenient when you are working on the same project for a while.

If you need to open another sketch, you either click the Open Sketch icon in the menu bar or select File ➤ Open. Alternatively, you can also select File ➤ Open Recent. This lists the last several sketches that you opened. Selecting one of these files opens it in a new instance of the IDE.

Board and Port Selection

Something that is crucial to the proper compiling and loading of a sketch is the selection of the appropriate board and port. Board and port selection is done from the Tools menu.

Selecting the board tells the compiler which version of Arduino you are using. As you grow in your Arduino, robotics, and/or IoT experience, you will likely use different boards. One of the great things about the Arduino IDE is its flexibility. You find yourself using the familiar and comfortable environment to program a great many different boards by different manufacturers. This lends to the adoption of Arduino as a de facto standard in the maker community.

To select the board and port for your robot, make sure that your Arduino is connected via USB, and the Arduino IDE is installed and opened.

1. Select **Tools ➤ Board** from the menu.

2. Select **Arduino/Genuino Uno** from the list of available boards.

3. Select **Tool ➤ Port** from the menu.

    There should be one entry in the list that says something like **Arduino/Genuino Uno on TTYAMC0**.

4. Select this entry.

At this point, the Arduino IDE should be ready to compile and load sketches to your board. We will write our first sketch to put it to the test shortly.

Cheating with Examples

When you install the Arduino IDE, you also install a collection of example sketches (see Figure 5-5). These are excellent reference for learning your way around Arduino coding. As you learning, look through these sketches for functionality that is similar to what you are trying to accomplish.

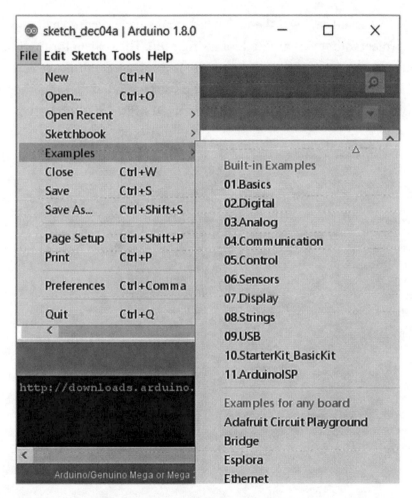

Figure 5-5. *List of example code included with the base install*

To view a list of examples or to open one, click File ➤ Examples. As you add more libraries (such as those for sensors and other devices), you add to this list of examples. So as you expand your own capabilities, as well as those of your robot, be sure to revisit the examples.

Using Tabs and Multiple Files

When I discussed saving a sketch earlier, it may have seemed a little odd that a project folder was created for a single file. The reason for this is a project can consist of more than one file. You can create multiple Arduino files for a project or you may want to keep your included files together with your project. Figure 5-6 shows the Arduino IDE with three tabs open.

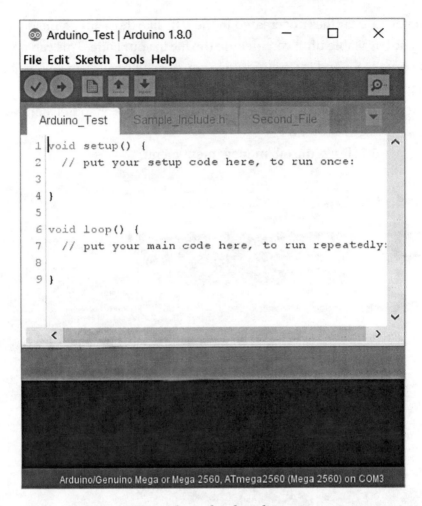

Figure 5-6. *Arduino IDE with multiple tabs*

When you have multiple code files in a project folder, each one appears as a tab in the Arduino IDE when you open a file in that project. This allows you to easily navigate between the files while you are working.

When working with tabs and multiple files, there are a few things to keep in mind. Code in tabs created through the IDE and saved as INO files is appended to the end of the main INO file. This means any functions you create in these tabs are available to use in any of these tabs.

However, tabs for files not created in the IDE, like those for an included file, is not available until you include the file in your code. This can be both convenient and frustrating since you need to track from which file a particular function comes.

I touch a little more on including files later in this chapter when we review coding in Arduino.

Figure 5-7 shows the tab management menu.

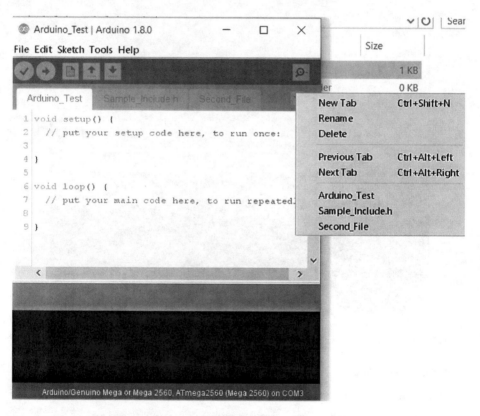

Figure 5-7. *Tab management menu*

You can create a new tab to help organize your code. When you create a new tab, that tab is saved as a new file within your project file.

1. Open the Arduino IDE and start a new file.

2. Save the file to create a new project file.

3. Click the arrow in the tab bar of the IDE.

4. Click **New Tab**.

5. In the dialog that opens, enter a name for your tab. Keep in mind that this is the name of the new file in your project folder.

6. Save the file. All unsaved tabs are also saved.

Once the tab is saved, Arduino automatically creates a new file to store the code in the tab.

Sketches

Programs for the Arduino are called *sketches*. The idea is that you are simply sketching code—as you would sketch an idea on a restaurant napkin. And, in all honesty, it does feel that way sometimes.

You are writing Arduino sketches in a language called Programming. It is a thin version of the C programming language designed to make coding easier. Arduino actually uses a modified version of Programming made for the Arduino board. It is essentially a reduced set of instructions that the AVR processor is able to run.

Like Python, you can add libraries as you add functionality and complexity. In C, we use the `include` directive. It serves the same purpose as the `import` command in Python. We'll see that in a little while when we do some communication between the two boards.

Hello Arduino

To understand the difference between programming Arduino and Python, we'll write a simple program. As with the chapter on GPIO, the first program is the hardware version of Hello World—a blinking LED. After you've loaded the program, you'll learn more about programming, its structure, and how to work with it.

In the GPIO chapter, we built a small circuit with an LED. The Arduino, however, has an LED built into the board that is available for our use, so we won't need to break out the breadboard just yet. The LED is attached to pin 13 on the UNO; it may differ on other versions.

1. Open the Arduino IDE from your programming menu.

2. Verify the board is connected and detected.

3. On the Arduino IDE menu, go to Tools and hover over **Board**. You should see **Arduino Uno** selected.

4. Now hover over Serial Port. It should say something like /dev/ttyUSB0. Yours may be different if your Pi assigned a different port. The point is that there's something there and it's checked.

5. Close the Tools menu by clicking somewhere outside the menu.

6. Enter the following code:

    ```
    int ledPin = 13;

    void setup() {
            pinMode(ledPin, OUTPUT);
    }
    ```

```
void loop() {
        digitalWrite(ledPin, HIGH);
        delay(1000);
        digitalWrite(ledPin, LOW);
        delay(1000);
}
```

7. Save the file as `blink_test`.

8. Click the check box icon to compile the sketch.

9. If you get any errors, make sure that you've entered the code correctly. Remember, unlike Python, you have to end each line with a semicolon. And like Python, capitalization matters.

10. When everything compiles correctly, click the arrow icon (pointing right). This uploads the sketch to the Arduino.

Wait a few seconds while it uploads. Afterward, you should see the LED connected to pin 13 blinking.

Congratulations, you just finished your first Arduino program. In addition, you did it from your Pi.

Anatomy of a Sketch

The sketch we just wrote is not the most complex, but it does illustrate the basic structure of an Arduino sketch.

```
int ledPin = 13;
```

We started by creating an integer variable, called `ledPin`, and assigned it the number 13. It's a good habit to give variables meaningful names, even when the program is short and only has one variable.

```
void setup() {
```

We then created a function called setup(). This function and the loop() function exist in every Arduino sketch. The setup function is where you put preparatory code, such as opening serial ports or, as we did in this sketch, define how we use pins. The setup function runs once, at the beginning of the program.

```
pinMode(ledPin, OUTPUT);
```

In the setup function, we have a single command. The pinMode function tells the compiler how a pin is used. In this case, we are declaring ledPin (with a value of 13) as an output pin. This tells the compiler that we are sending out signals, and we are not expecting to receive signals through this pin.

We then close the setup function with the closing parenthesis before starting our loop function.

```
void loop() {
```

The loop function is the only other required element of an Arduino sketch. As the name suggests, loop is run continuously and repeatedly until power is removed from the board, or the board is reset. It is the equivalent of the while true: command in Python. Any code in the loop function is repeated as quickly as the processor can manage.

```
digitalWrite(ledPin, HIGH);
```

Within the loop function, we have the code to blink our LED. We start by setting the pin to a high state with the digitalWrite function. Again, we pass it ledPin and the state we want to set—in this case, HIGH.

```
delay(1000);
```

The next line adds a 1,000 millisecond, or one-second, delay before executing the next command.

```
digitalWrite(ledPin, LOW);
```

After the one second delay, we set the pin to a low state using the same command used to set it high, `digitalWrite`. This time, however, we pass it the constant LOW.

```
delay(1000);
```

Again, we introduce a one-second delay. Because this is the last command in the `loop` function, after the delay we return to the start of the `loop` function. This continues until we unplug the Arduino or upload another sketch.

A Brief Introduction to the Arduino Language

As discussed earlier, the Arduino programming language is derived from the Programming language. Programming, in turn, has its roots in C. If you are familiar with coding in C, the Arduino is easy to work with. Many of the functions, syntax, and shortcuts work as well in Arduino as in C.

For the rest, you catch on pretty quickly. Keep in mind, Arduino is not Python and behaves much differently when you are working with it.

For instance, Arduino is much less concerned with white space and formatting than Python, where indentation is used to denote blocks of code. In C, blocks of code are defined using curly braces {}. That being said, you cannot ignore white space all together. An extra space at the beginning of a line can cause no end of frustration.

Another key difference that frustrates beginners and seasoned programmers, alike, is line termination. In Python, you simply move to the next line, no terminator needed. However, in Arduino and C, lines are terminated with a semicolon. If a semicolon is not present where the compiler expects it, you get an error. This is the single most common error beginners make. If your code won't compile, the first thing to look for is a missing semicolon.

One thing shared between Python and Arduino is case sensitivity. It is important to remember case matters. `intPin` is not the same as `intpin`. This is the second thing to look for if your code doesn't compile properly or behave as expected.

Including Other Files

Much like Python, there are times when you need to include other files or libraries. This is most likely when you add sensors, motors, or other devices to the Arduino and need to add the device's library to your code.

Arduino uses the C and C++ method of adding code from external files through the `#include` directive. The following line includes the standard servo library:

```
#include <Servo.h>
```

Like all directives, `include` has a slightly different syntax. Note that there is no semicolon at the end of this line. A semicolon causes an error, and the code will not compile. Also, the `include` keyword is preceded by a # (hash).

Variables and Data Types

Like Python, Arduino has all the common data types, although they may act a little bit different. One of the biggest differences between Python and Arduino is that you must declare your variable before you use it. A good example is the `for` loop. In Python, you could do something like this:

```
for i in range (0, 3):
```

In C and Arduino, the loop looks like this:

```
for (int i = 0; i < 3; i ++) {... }
```

These are wildly different statements. I explain the `for` loop syntax later in this chapter.

The key thing to observe here is that in Python, the i variable is created without a type and becomes an integer when the first value, 0, is assigned to it. In Arduino, you have to tell the compiler what the variable is before you assign a value to it; otherwise, you receive an error similar to this:

```
Error: variable i not defined in this scope
```

The rules for declaring variables are the same as for Python, and the best practices are also the same.

- Variables can only contain letters, numbers, and underscores.

- They are case sensitive; variable is not the same as Variable. That's going to bite you later.

- Don't use Python keywords.

- Make the variable name meaningful with as few characters as possible.

- Be careful when using lowercase L and uppercase O, which look very similar to 1 and 0, and can lead to confusion. I'm not saying don't use them; just make sure that it's clear what you're doing. Using them as single character variable names is strongly discouraged.

Characters and Strings

Strings come in three flavors; characters, strings as arrays of characters, and strings as objects. Each of these is handled in distinctly different manners.

A character (char) is a single alphanumeric character stored as an ASCII numeric value. Remember, computers work on 1s and 0s, and everything eventually gets broken down into numbers stored as 1s and 0s. ASCII codes are the numeric values that represent individual alphanumeric characters. For instance, the letter a is actually ASCII code 97.

Even invisible characters have ASCII representation. The ASCII code for carriage return is 13. You frequently see these written using the same notation as the char function, such as char(13).

A string of characters can be handled in two different ways. The native method for handling strings inherited from C is the array of chars. You declare this type of string like this:

```
string someWord[7];
```

Or

```
string someWord[] = "Arduino";
```

This creates a string consisting of 10 characters stored as an array. We'll learn more about arrays shortly, but they are roughly the equivalent of Python lists. To access a character in a string of this type, you use its position in the array. The someWord[0] example returns the character A.

The String Object

Although there may be times that you want to manipulate characters and character strings in the way that I just explained, Arduino provides a much more convenient way of working with strings: the String object. Note the capital S.

The String object provides a number of built in methods for working with text and converting other values into a string. Many of these functions are easily recreated using simple array manipulation. The String object simply makes it easier; however, if you are not planning to do a lot of string manipulation, this may be overkill.

Examples of functions useful for string manipulation are trim(), toUpperCase(), and toLowerCase().

There are several ways to create a String object. Because it is an object, you have to create an instance of the String object. An object is generally instantiated the same way you declare any other variable.

In fact, since all data types are essentially objects, it is exactly the same. For instance, this is how you initiate an instance of a `String` object called `myString`:

```
String myString;
```

Or

```
String myString = "Arduino";
```

Numbers

Like Python, there are several number formats available. The most common are the integer (`int`) and the decimal (float). You occasionally use Boolean types and a few others.

An integer represents a 16-bit number between –32,768 to 32,767. An unsigned integer can hold a positive value between 0 and 65,535. A long integer (long) is a 32-bit number from –2,147,483,648 to 2,147,483,647. So depending on the size of the number that you need, you have a few options.

Decimals, or non-whole numbers, are stored as float types. A *float* is 32-bit number from –3.4028235E+38 to 3.4028235E+38. Like Python, floats in Arduino are not native and are only approximate. But they are more precise in Arduino than in Python.

The following code illustrates how to create number variables in Arduino:

```
int myNumber;
int myNumber = 10;
long myLongInt;
long myLongInt = 123456;
float myFloat;
float myFloat = 10.1;
```

Be sure to note the semicolon at the end of each line. Every line of code, with the exception of code blocks, must be terminated with a semicolon.

Arrays

As mentioned earlier, an array is essentially the same as a list in Python. They are denoted with brackets ([ ]). Addressing a value within an array works exactly as it does in Python. Arduino arrays are also zero based, which means the first value in the array is at position 0.

The following example creates an array, iterates through them, and then outputs some of the values to the serial port.

1. Create a new sketch in the Arduino IDE.

2. Save the sketch as `array_example`.

3. Update the code to look like this:

```
int numbers[5];
int moreNumbers[5] = {1,2,3,4,5};

void setup() {
   // put your setup code here, to run once:
Serial.begin(9600);
}

void loop() {
   // put your main code here, to run repeatedly:
for(int i = 0; i < 5; i++){
   Serial.println(numbers[i]);
   }

for(int i = 0; i < 5; i++){
   numbers[i] = moreNumbers[i];
}

for(int i = 0; i < 5; i++){
   Serial.println(numbers[i]);
   }
```

```
numbers[1] = 12;

for(int i = 0; i < 5; i++){
  Serial.println(numbers[i]);
  }
}
```

4. Save the file.

5. Upload the sketch to your Arduino.

6. Click **Tools ➤ Serial Monitor**.

Control Structures

Like Python, Arduino provides several structures to add some control to your code. These should be fairly familiar since they are very similar to their counterparts in Python. Of course, syntax is different, and you'll need to pay attention to your semicolons and brackets.

if and else

This is generally considered the most basic construct. It simply allows you to execute code based on the results of a Boolean condition. If the condition evaluates to true, then the code executes; otherwise, the program skips the code and executes the next command. Here is an example of an if statement:

```
if(val == 1){doSomething();}
```

In this example, we are simply evaluating the contents of the val variable. If val contains the integer 1, then the code within the brackets is executed; otherwise, the program skips the code and continues with the next line.

The entire clause does not need to be, and most frequently is not confined to a single line. Generally, even if the code within the brackets consists of a single line, I expand the statement to use multiple lines. I just find this easier to read. This code is functionally identical to the previous example.

```
if(val == 1){
        doSomething();
        }
```

You can evaluate for multiple values using the else statement, which works exactly as you would expect it to. You are simply telling the compiler to evaluate each consecutive condition if the previous condition evaluates to false.

```
if(val == 1){
        doSomething();
}
else if(val == 2){
        doSomethingElse();
}
else if(otherVal == 3){
        doAnotherThing();
}
else {
        doAlternateThing();
}
```

The first part of this code is the same as the earlier examples. If the value of val is 1, then do something. If this condition is false, val is not 1, then check to see if it is 2. If so, do something else. If that is also not true, then check the value of otherVal. If that is 3, then do another thing. Lastly, if none of the previous conditions is true, then execute this code.

The final else statement is not necessary. You could leave this statement out, and the code would just continue running whatever code follows. The final else statement is for code you only want to run if all the other conditions are not true.

Also, take note of the second else/if statement. You do not have to evaluate the same variable for another condition. Any operation that evaluates to true or false is valid.

while Loops

while loops repeatedly execute a block of code as long as a condition is true. In Python, we used this to create a continuous loop to execute our programing constantly. That practice is not necessary in Arduino since the standard Loop() function provides that functionality.

Like the if statement, while evaluates a condition. If the condition evaluates to true, the code block is executed. Once the code block executes, it evaluates the condition again. If the condition still evaluates to true, the code block is executed again. This continues until the condition evaluates to false. Because of this, it is very important to make sure that the value evaluated in the condition is updated in the code block.

This is an example of a while loop:

```
int i = 0;

while(i < 3){
        doSomething();
        i++;
}
```

In this example, we create an integer with the value 0 before we enter the while loop. The while statement evaluates the value i. Since it is currently 0, which is less than 3, it executes the code block. Within the code block we increment the value if i. The while statement evaluates the value again. This time it is 1, which is still less than 3, so the code block is again executed. This continues until the value of i is incremented to 3. Since 3 is not less than 3, the while loop exits without executing the code block.

Like all the other loops, the while loop is blocking. This means as long as the condition evaluates to true, the code block executes, preventing any other code from being executed.

This feature is commonly used to prevent code from running until a condition is present in order to prevent errors or unexpected results later. For instance, if your code requires a serial connection to be present before it can continue, you might add this code to your program:

```
Serial.begin(9600);
while(!Serial){}
```

The Serial function is part of the standard Arduino library. It simply checks to see if a serial connection is available. If a serial connection has been established, Serial evaluates to true. However, the exclamation point (!) preceding it means *not*. So we are saying, "As long as there is no serial connection, execute this code." The code block is empty, so there is no code to run. The result is that the code stops until a serial connection is available.

for Loops

Like the while loop, the for loop executes a code block repeatedly until the condition evaluates to true. The difference between the two is that a for loop also defines and transforms the variable being evaluated. Generally, this is simply setting up an integer to serve as a counter, evaluating the value against a set threshold, and incrementing the value. With each increment, the code block is executed until the condition no longer evaluates to true; for example:

```
for(int i = 0; i < 3; i++){
        doSomething();
}
```

In this example, we declare an integer called i. We want to continue to loop the code block as long as i is less than 3. Every time we execute the code, we increment the value of i by 1 until the value of i is 3. Since 3 is not less than 3, the loop exits without executing the code block.

This is useful for when you want to execute a piece of code a specific number of times. You can also use the value being incremented. For instance, if we wanted an LED on pin 13 to fade on rather than simply turning on, we could this code:

```
pinMode(11, OUTPUT);
for(int i = 0; i < 255; i++){
        analogWrite(11, i);
}
```

First, we tell the Arduino that we want to use pin 13 as an output pin. You learn more about working with pins shortly. Then we set up our for loop to increment the value of i from 0 to 254. The value of i is then written to pin 13, setting the PWM value. If you recall from the previous chapter, the PWM value controls the brightness of the LED by determining how often the pin is high in a given cycle. Thus, we have an LED that increases to its maximum brightness.

We actually write the LED fading code when we start working with pins.

Functions

Like Python, the Arduino allows you to break you code up into smaller parts through functions. An Arduino function is very similar to one in Python. The syntax, of course, is different. But, with both, you declare the function name, list any parameters needed, and provide a block of code to execute when the function is called.

You are already familiar with the syntax of an Arduino function. Both the setup and loop blocks in an Arduino sketch are functions. The only difference is that these are system functions that are automatically called as appropriate during runtime. If you are familiar with C or C++, they are similar to the main() function at the root of those languages.

You use a function anytime you have a block of code that you may want to use in more than one place. This way, you write it only once, and it always performs the same regardless of where you call it from.

The general syntax of a function looks like this:

```
returnType functionName(parameterType parameterName){
        doSomething();
}
```

It's probably better and easier to walk you through the creation and use of a function.

In this exercise, we create a simple function that adds two numbers together. It's not a particularly practical function, but it provides an example of how to go about creating a function.

1. Create a new sketch in the Arduino IDE.

2. Save the sketch as `function_example`.

3. Update the code to this:

```
int a = 1;
int b = 2;
int val;
int answer;

int add_vars(){
  val = a+b;
  return val;
}
int add_params(int p1, int p2){
  val = p1+p2;
  return val;
}
```

```
void printVal(){
  Serial.println(val);
}

void setup() {
  // put your setup code here, to run once:
  Serial.begin(9600);
}

void loop() {
  // put your main code here, to run repeatedly:
  add_vars();
  printVal();

  add_params(a,b);
  printVal();

  answer = add_vars();
  Serial.println(answer);

  a++;
  b++;
}
```

4. Upload the sketch to your Arduino.

5. Open the serial monitor from the Tools menu.

In this exercise, we created three functions. The first two functions return a value of type int. As such, we precede the function's name with the data type int. The third function does not return data; it simply performs a task, so it is preceded with void.

The first function, add_vars(), adds two global variables together. This emphasizes both the benefit and danger of global variables. A global variable can be manipulated by any code in your program. This is an easy method to perform tasks on the same data, and then pass that data from one function to another. However, you must be aware that any changes you make to the variable applies everywhere that variable is used.

A safer alternative to this is to use parameters in your function. In this way, you have more control since you are providing the values. The second function, add_params(), demonstrates this. The parameters are created as part of the function declaration. We provide the data type for each one and the variable name to be used within the function. So, it is exactly like declaring a variable, except the value is assigned at runtime when the function is called.

The last function returns no data and requires no parameters. In this particular case, we are printing the value of the global variable val to the serial port.

Working with Pins

The primary purpose of the Arduino is to interface with other components, sensors, or other devices. To do this, we'll need to know how to interact with the pins. The pins of the Arduino connect directly to the AVR processor at its heart.

The Arduino provides access to 14 digital pins, 6 analog pins, 6 hardware PWM pins, TTL serial, SPI, and two-wire serial. I put emphasis on hardware PWM because any of the digital or analog pins can be used for software PWM. I don't cover all of these capabilities in this book, but I recommend that you take the time to learn about them.

We are going to look at your basic digital and analog inputs and outputs. These are the functions that you use most often.

Before you can use any of the pins as input or output, you must first declare how you use it. This is done using the pinMode() function. To do this, all you have to do is provide the pin number and the mode. For example, this code sets pin 13 as an output pin:

```
pinMode(13, OUTPUT);
```

I frequently use a variable for the pin number. This makes it easier to identify what you're doing in the code; for example:

```
int servoPin = 11;
int LEDPin = 13;
```

Now, when I need to reference a pin, it's easier to understand.

```
pinMode(LEDPin, OUTPUT);
```

Digital Operations

Now that we have the pin defined, we can start using it.

As with Python, you can turn a pin on or off by setting it either high or low. This is done using the `digitalWrite()` function, with which you supply the pin number and either high or low; for example:

```
digitalWrite(LEDPin, HIGH);
```

Using the `pinMode()` example, this turns pin 13 high, or on.

Likewise, you can turn a pin off by setting it low.

On the other side, you can read the current state of a pin with `digitalRead()`. To do this, you first have to set the mode to input.

```
int buttonPin = 3;
int val;
pinMode(buttonPin, INPUT);
val = digitalRead(buttonPin);
```

This code snippet assigns the value 3 to the `buttonPin` variable, and we create a variable to store the results. It then sets the pins mode to input so that we can read it. Finally, we read the value of pin 13 into the `val` variable.

Analog Input

Analog input works a little different; although you can use any IO pin for digital operations, you can only use designated analog pins for analog input. As I discussed in the introduction to Python, microcontrollers cannot truly do analog. One way or another the signal must be converted between analog and digital. With analog output, this is done via pulse width modulation (PWM). For analog input, we use an analog to digital converter, or ADC, to convert an analog signal into a digital one. This is a hardware function, and so it must be performed on specific pins. In the case of the Arduino Uno, these pins are A0 to A5.

Since these pins are dedicated to analog input, declaring them as input is not strictly necessary. I still recommend doing so because it serves as an indication that these pins are in use.

The `analogRead()` function is used to read the pins; for example:

```
val = analogRead(A0);
```

This assigns the value of A0 to the variable `val`. This is an integer value between 0 and 1023.

Analog Output (PWM)

PWM works much the same as it does in Python. On designated pins, you can provide a value between 0 and 255 to vary the output of the pin. A value of 0 is the analog equivalent of digital low, or off; whereas a value of 255 is analogous to digital high, or on. As such, a value of 127 provides a 50% duty cycle, roughly the same as half power.

With the Arduino, you use `analogWrite()` to set the PWM signal of a pin. On the Arduino Uno, the PWM pins are 5, 11, 12, 15, 16, and 17. The following code snippet sets the output of pin 11 to approximately 25%.

```
int PWMPin = 11;
pinMode(PWMPin, OUTPUT);
analogWrite(PWMPin, 64);
```

Pulsing LED

In this exercise, we are going make an LED pulse. Pin 13 is not a PWM pin, so we won't be able to use the built in LED this time, which means that it's time to breakout the breadboard and a few jumpers.

The Circuit

To connect the circuit, we need a 220-ohm resistor, a 5V LED, your Arduino, breadboard, and a few jumpers. See Figure 5-8 to wire up this exercise.

1. Connect the LED to the breadboard.

2. Connect the resistor such that one end is connected to the channel shared with the long pin of the LED.

3. Connect a jumper from the other pin of the diode to the GND pin on the Arduino.

4. Connect a jumper from the other end of the resistor to pin 11 on the Arduino.

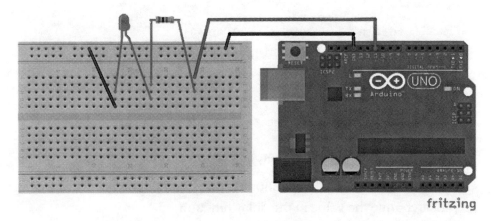

Figure 5-8. *LED fade exercise circuit layout*

The Code

Earlier we used `analogWrite()` in a for loop example. Now we write the code to implement the example on the Arduino.

1. Create a new sketch in the Arduino IDE.

2. Save the sketch as `PWM_Example`.

3. Update the code to this:

```
int PWMPin = 11;

void setup() {
  // put your setup code here, to run once:
  pinMode(PWMPin, OUTPUT);
}

void loop() {
  // put your main code here, to run repeatedly:
  for(int i = 0; i < 255; i++){
    analogWrite(PWMPin, i);
  }

  for(int i = 255; i >= 0; i--){
    analogWrite(PWMPin, i);
  }
  delay(100);
}
```

4. Save and upload the sketch to your Arduino.

The LED on the breadboard should now pulse. To change the rate of the pulse, change the value in the delay function.

Objects and Classes

Creating objects and classes is beyond the scope of this book. You very rarely, if ever, need to create one within Arduino. You frequently use objects or classes from other libraries, however.

An object is generally instantiated the same way that you declare any other variable; you tell the compiler the type of object followed by the name of the variable referring to it.

```
ObjectType variableName;
```

Once declared, you have access to all the properties and methods of this class. A good example of this is the Servo class. This is a standard library with Arduino. The following code snippet creates a servo object and attaches it to pin 12:

```
#include <Servo.h>

Servo myServo;
myServo.attach(12);
```

First, we include the Servo library. Once the Servo library is included, we can easily create an instance of the Servo class. In this case, we create a servo object called myServo. Once the object is created, we can use the attach() method to assign pin 12 to control the servo.

Serial

There are a couple of serial channels on the Arduino. We use the USB connection between the Raspberry Pi and the Arduino. This is by far the simplest way to communicate between the two.

167

Connecting to Serial

To use serial communication, you must first initiate it. To do this, use
`Serial.begin(baudRate)`. For example, this line initiates the serial
connection with a baud rate of 9600bps:

```
Serial.begin(9600);
```

The baud rate you choose is entirely up to you and your needs. The
important thing is that is matches the baud rate of the computer is connected
to. So, when you initialize the serial connection on the Pi, you'll need to
make sure that they match. I'll discuss establishing that connection shortly.

To verify the serial connection was successful, you can query the
`Serial` keyword. Serial is a Boolean object that indicates whether or not
a serial connection is available. If a connection is available, it is true;
otherwise, it's false. There are actually a few ways to use `Serial`. You can
use it as the Boolean condition for an `if` statement and put the dependent
code in the `if` statement's code block. Alternatively, you can use it as the
Boolean condition of a `while` loop.

Here are two methods to check for a serial connection. Only run the
code if one is available.

```
if(Serial){
        doSomething();
}

while(Serial){
        doSomething();
}
```

The first block executes the code if a serial connection is available,
and then moves on to the code following the `if` statement. The second
block runs the code continuously, as long as a connection is available. Any
code following the `while` loop will not run until the serial connection is
terminated and the loop is exited.

168

A third alternative is to halt the running of all code while a connection is not available. This is another while loop that we've seen before.

```
while(!Serial){}
```

This uses the "not" operator, or exclamation mark (!). In order for the condition to evaluate to true it must not meet the criteria. In this case, as long as a connection is not available, execute the code in the block. But, since there is no code, it simply halts the program until one is available.

Sending Serial Data

Much of what we'll do is simply printing to the serial port. In fact, that's what we've been doing in earlier examples. The method Serial.println() sends the data within the parenthesis to the serial port. The serial monitor in the Arduino IDE allows you to see this output.

To write data to the serial stream, you generally use one of the serial print methods. Serial.print() prints the contents of the parentheses to the serial stream without a new line terminator. This means that everything you print using this method appears on the same line in the serial monitor.

The Serial.println() method includes the new line terminator. So everything printed with this method is followed by a new line.

Receiving Serial Data

Of course, the serial port works the other way, too. You can read the serial stream from the Pi using several methods of the Serial object. Many of the methods to read data from serial are for working with the individual bytes. This can be confusing and cumbersome if you're just getting started. If you are familiar and comfortable working with individual bytes of data, Serial.read(), Serial.readByte(), and others are probably useful.

However, that is not what we'll use. To make things a little bit easier, we'll use the Serial.parseInt() and Serial.readString() methods.

Both of these methods do the lion's share of the work when reading from the serial stream.

Serial.parseInt() reads through the incoming serial stream and returns; however, it does not parse the integers all at once. When you first call it, it returns the first integer it encounters. The next call returns the next integer. Each iteration returns the next integer found until it reaches the end of the line.

Let's take a look at how parseInt() works. In the following code, the Arduino waits to receive input from the serial stream. It then iterates through the input and parses out the integers, printing each one on a new line.

1.   Open a new sketch in the Arduino IDE.

2.   Save the sketch as parseInt_example.

3.   Enter the this code:

```
int val;

void setup() {
  // put your setup code here, to run once:
  Serial.begin(9600);
}

void loop() {
  // put your main code here, to run repeatedly:
  while(Serial.available() > 0){
    val = Serial.parseInt();
    Serial.println(val);
  }
}
```

4.   Upload the sketch to your Arduino.

5.   Open the serial monitor.

6. In the data entry field at the top of the serial monitor, enter **1,2,3,4**. Be sure to separate each value with a comma.

7. Click **Send**.

The serial monitor writes each integer on a new line. If you enter an alpha character, it prints a 0 since it is an alphanumeric character but not an integer.

`Serial.readString()` reads the entire line from the serial stream as a string. This can be assigned to a `String` variable for later use. This method works well if you are sending text information to the Arduino. However, it is slow, and you notice significant lag between the time that a line is sent and the time that it is received, processed, and available.

Arduino to Pi and Back Again

You need to know a bit about serial communication because it is how we communicate between the Raspberry Pi and the Arduino. Both the Pi and Arduino work with serial communications differently.

I did not cover serial in the Python chapter because it is important that this discussion occur in conjunction with the Arduino. As such, you may want to jump back to Chapter 3 for a quick review of Python after all of that Arduino coding.

I have talked about how to open a serial connection on the Arduino. The Raspberry Pi is just a touch more complicated. First, serial communications is not part of the default framework. So, we need to install it. Once installed, our code needs to import the serial library. Once that is done, we create an instance of the serial class, which gives us access to the methods that we need.

Installing PySerial

Serial functionality is provided by the PySerial package. To use it, you first need to make sure that it is installed in your Python implementation.

1. On your Raspberry Pi, open a terminal window.

2. Type **python -m pip install pyserial**.

   This installs the PySerial package if it is not already installed.

3. Type **python**.

   This begins a new Python session within the terminal.

4. Type **import serial**.

   This verifies your version of PySerial.

Now that PySerial is installed, we can use it in our programs.

To use serial in Python, we need to import the library and create a connection. The following code snippet is likely in most of the scripts that interact with the Arduino:

```
import serial
ser = serial.Serial('/dev/ttyAMC0', 9600)
```

Creating a serial connection in Python is similar to what we did with the Arduino. The biggest difference is we assigned the serial object to a variable; in this case, ser. In the initiation call, we provide the port the Arduino is on as well as the baud rate at which we are connecting. Again, make sure that this matches the baud rate you set on the Arduino. If these don't match, you get odd characters and unexpected results—if you get anything at all.

Sending Data to the Raspberry Pi

It is not so much about sending data to the Pi as much as it is about how the Pi receives the data and then what it does with it.

The simplest approach to receiving serial data on the Pi is to use the readLine() method of the serial object. This reads the bytes from the serial stream until it reaches the new line character. The bytes are then converted to a string. All the data sent on the line is stored in a single string. Depending on how you are sending your data from the Arduino, you may then need to use the split() method to parse the data into a tuple.

It is important to note that the readLine() method continues to read the serial stream until a new line character is received. If you do not send one from the Arduino, the Pi continues to try to read the data. To help prevent locking your program, you may want to set the timeout interval prior to attempting the readLine(). This can be accomplished by adding the timeout parameter when you create the connection. The following line of code creates the serial connection with a one-second timeout:

```
ser = serial.Serial('/dev/ttyAMC0', 9600, timeout=1)
```

My preferred method of sending data between the Pi and the Arduino is through a series of comma-separated values. Depending on the complexity of the project, I may either do a direct read, where each value passed corresponds to a specific variable. This has the benefit of being pretty straightforward. All I have to do is parse the serial stream into integers and assign each integer, in order, to their respective variable for later use.

On more complex projects, I may send values in pairs or sets of integers. When parsed, the first integer usually indicates the function or the device the message is for; the second is the value to assign to the variable.

From the Arduino, I simply write the values and their comma separators in a number of Serial.print() commands terminated with a Serial.println() to make sure that the line is properly terminated.

On the Pi, I use the readLine() method to capture the entire line as a single string then use the split() method to parse the string into a tuple. The tuple could be further parsed into individual variables as needed.

To illustrate this, let's create a simple program that sends a sequence of numbers from the Arduino to the Raspberry Pi every 500 milliseconds. This is frequent enough to not timeout.

On the Pi, we parse those values and assign them to individual variables. This is a common use-case to send sensor readings from the Arduino to the Pi.

To do this, we have to write two programs: one for the Arduino and one for the Pi. Let's start on the Arduino.

1. Create a new sketch in the Arduino IDE.

2. Save the sketch as Arduino_to_Pi_example.

3. Enter the following code:

```
int a = 1;
int b = 2;
int c = 3;

void setup() {
  // put your setup code here, to run once:
  Serial.begin(9600);
}

void loop() {
  // put your main code here, to run repeatedly:
  while(!Serial){};
  Serial.print(a); Serial.print(",");
  Serial.print(b); Serial.print(",");
  Serial.println(c);
```

```
    delay(500);
    a++;
    b++;
    c++;
}
```

4. Save and upload the sketch to your Arduino.

5. Open a new Python file in IDLE.

6. Save the file as Arduino_to_pi_example.py.

7. Enter the following code:

```
import serial

ser = serial.Serial('/dev/ttyACM0',9600,timeout=1)

while 1:
    val = ser.readline().decode('utf-8')
    parsed = val.split(',')
    parsed = [x.rstrip() for x in parsed]
    if(len(parsed) > 2):
        print(parsed)
        a = int(int(parsed[0]+'0')/10)
        b = int(int(parsed[1]+'0')/10)
        c = int(int(parsed[2]+'0')/10)
    print(a)
    print(b)
    print(c)
    print(a+b+c)
```

8. Save and run the file.

In the IDLE shell window, you should see output similar to this:

```
['1','2','3']
1
2
3
6
```

We did some Python magic in here that we need to review.

First, we imported the serial library and opened a serial connection. Once the connection was opened, we entered the perpetual while loop. After that, I introduced a few new elements that I want to walk through,

```
val = ser.readline().decode('utf-8')
```

We read the next line coming from the serial stream. However, this string is retrieved as a byte string, which works differently than a standard string. To make it easier to use, we used the decode() method to convert the string from a byte string to a standard string. This allows us to use methods of the string class to work with the line.

```
parsed = val.split(',')
```

Next, we parsed the string into a list. Since we used commas to separate our numbers from the Arduino, provide that to the split() method. However, now the last element in the list includes the end of line characters /n/r. We don't want those characters.

```
parsed = [x.rstrip() for x in parsed]
```

This line rebuilds the parsed list without the extra characters. The rstrip() method removes any white space from the string. So, what this line does is loop through each member of the list and applies the rstrip() method. We are left with a list of number as strings.

```
if(len(parsed) > 2):
```

One of the challenges we are going to face with serial communications between the two boards is packet loss. This is particularly prevalent when we reset Arduino, which occurs every time we make a new serial connection. This loss results in missing characters in the serial string.

To overcome this challenge in this script we test the length of the list. The len() function returns the number of members in a list. Since we know our list needs to contain, at least, three numbers, we only want to run the remaining code if this condition is true.

```
print(parsed)
```

This line simply prints the parsed list to the shell window.

```
a = int(int(parsed[0]+'0')/10)
b = int(int(parsed[1]+'0')/10)
c = int(int(parsed[2]+'0')/10)
```

The last piece of Python magic was done when we assigned the values to their respective variables. These lines include both string and numeric manipulation.

To read what's going on here we have to start in the middle where we add the '0' character to the end of each list member. We did this because, despite our earlier efforts, there may still be empty strings in the list. Empty strings cannot be converted to an integer and the code will not compile. By adding the 0, we are assured that there is an actual value there.

We then convert that string to an integer. However, that integer now has a 0 appended to the end, making 1 read as 10, and so forth. To adjust for this, we divide that number by 10, which results in a float. Since we are looking for an integer, we have to convert the final results to an int.

The last part of the code is simply printing the value of each variable to the shell window. The last line is included to prove that we are operating with integers and not strings.

Sending Data to the Arduino

To send data to the Arduino is a fairly simple matter, on the Arduino side. Python is a touch more involved, however. Using the same scenario as earlier, we need to put the values into a tuple, and then use the join() method to merge the values in the tuple into a single string. That string is then written to the serial connection.

On the Arduino, all we have to do is use parseInt() to break the string into the three independent integers, once again.

In this exercise, we are going to send three integers to the Arduino. In a real world scenario, these numbers might represent the color or brightness of an LED or an angle for a servo. However, it is going to be difficult to verify what is happening on the Arduino side because we can't use the serial monitor. To overcome this, we are going to ask the Arduino to sum the integers together and return the result to the Pi. This means that both boards are reading and writing to the serial stream.

Again, let's start on the Arduino side.

1. Open a new sketch in the Arduino IDE.

2. Save the sketch as roundtrip_example.

3. Enter the following code:

```
int a = 0;
int b = 0;
int c = 0;
int d = 0;
void setup() {
  // put your setup code here, to run once:
  Serial.begin(9600);
}
```

```
void loop() {
  // put your main code here, to run repeatedly:
  while(!Serial){}
  if(Serial.available()>0){
    a = Serial.parseInt();
    b = Serial.parseInt();
    c = Serial.parseInt();
  }

  d = a+b+c;
  Serial.print(a); Serial.print(",");
  Serial.print(b); Serial.print(",");
  Serial.print(c); Serial.print(",");
  Serial.println(d);

  //delay(500);
}
```

4. Save the sketch and upload it to your Arduino.

5. Open a new Python file in IDLE.

6. Save the file as roundtrip_example.py.

7. Enter the following code:

```
import serial
import time

ser = serial.Serial('/dev/ttyACM0',9600,timeout=1)
a = 1
b = 2
c = 3
```

```
    while 1:
        valList = [str(a),str(b),str(c)]
        sendStr = ','.join(valList)

        print(sendStr)

        ser.write(sendStr.encode('utf-8'))

        time.sleep(0.1)

        recStr = ser.readline().decode('utf-8')
        print(recStr)

        a = a+1
        b = b+1
        c = c+1
```

8. Save and run the file.

In the Python shell window, you should see output like this:

```
1,2,3
1,2,3,6
```

The output continues to increment until you stop the program.

There are a few new elements here, but, for the most part, it's not that different than we've done before. Let's look at some of the new elements.

The first difference is we imported the time library. This library provides a lot of time related functionality. In this exercise, we are interested in the sleep() function. The sleep() function pauses processing for the number of seconds provided. As you can see in our code, we wanted to pause processing for 0.5 seconds. This gives both sides of the serial stream time to process their buffers. If you comment out that line and run the program again, you'll get some interesting results. Try it.

```
valList = [str(a),str(b),str(c)]
```

Here we take our variables and put them in a list. In the next step, when we join the elements into a single string, the integers need be strings. So, we went ahead and did the conversion here.

```
sendStr = ','.join(valList)
```

Next, we used the join() method of the string class to convert the list into a string. Notice how the join() method is attached to the ',' string. join is a method of the string class, not the list class, so you have to call it from a string. Since the operation is actually working on a list, not a string, you have to provide a string for it to work. In this case, the provided string is the separator that you want between each member of the list. It can be any character, but for parseInt() to work on the Arduino side, the character has to be non-alphanumeric.

```
ser.write(sendStr.encode('utf-8'))
```

The other difference of note is where we send the data to the Arduino using the write() method. This works like the Serial.println() method in Arduino. The biggest difference is you have to encode the string before you can send it over.

Pinguino

A common use-case for attaching one or more sensors to detect the world around the robot. For the next exercise, we are going to set up our HC-SR04 ultrasonic rangefinder on the Arduino and send the distance information back to the Pi as a serial string. To do this, we need to open up a serial connection between the two boards. The Arduino triggers the sensor, and, as in our previous workshop, reads the pulse returned. We'll calculate the distance, and then send the result to the Pi.

On the Pi side, we'll simply have a program that listens to the serial port and then prints whatever it reads from the Arduino.

Setting up the Circuit

Setting up the circuit couldn't be easier. In fact, we don't use the breadboard. We're going to connect the sensor directly to the Arduino headers (see Figure 5-9).

1. Connect VCC to the 5V pin on the Arduino.

2. Connect GND to one of the GND pins on the Arduino. It doesn't matter which one, but there are two adjacent to the 5V pin.

3. Connect TRIG to pin 7 on the Arduino.

4. Connect ECHO to pin 8 on the Arduino.

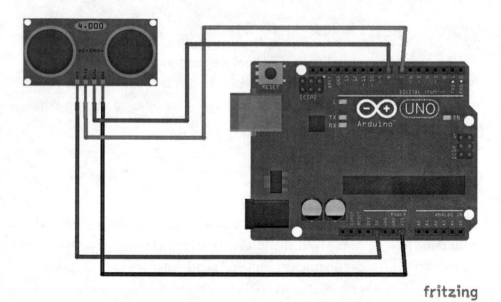

Figure 5-9. Pinguino exercise circuit layout

The Code

We need to write code for both boards in order for this to work. On the Arduino, we trigger the ultrasonic sensor and capture the return signal. We'll then convert it to centimeters and print the value to the serial port.

The Pi reads the line from the serial port and prints the results to the Python shell window.

Arduino

1. Open a new sketch window and save it as serial_test.

2. Enter the following code:

```
int trig = 7;
int echo = 8;
int duration = 0;
int distance = 0;

void setup() {
        Serial.begin(9600);
        pinMode(trig, OUTPUT);
        pinMode(echo, INPUT);

        digitalWrite(trig,LOW);
}

void loop() {
        digitalWrite(trig, HIGH);
        delayMicroseconds(10);
        digitalWrite(trig, LOW);
```

```
            duration = pulseIn(echo, HIGH);
            distance = duration/58.2;

            Serial.write(distance);

            delay(500);
        }
```

Save and upload the sketch to the Arduino.

Raspberry Pi

1. Open a new IDLE file and save it as serial_test.py.

2. Enter the following code:

```
import serial
import time

ser = serial.Serial('/dev/ttyAMC0', 9600)

while 1:
        recSer = ser.readline().decode('utf-8')
        recSer.rstrip()

        distance = int(recSer + '0')/10

        print("Distance: " + str(distance) + "cm      ",
        end = '\r')
        time.sleep(0.5)
```

3. Save and run the file.

You should now see text in the Python shell window with the distance in centimeters.

This code outputs the results from a single ultrasonic sensor. In reality, your robot should have three or more of these sensors pointing forward at different angles. The reason being, ultrasonic sensors work great as long as the obstacle is directly in front of the robot. If the robot approaches a wall or other obstacle at an oblique angle, the sound does not bounce back to the sensor. Having more than one sensor at different angles allows the robot to detect obstacles that are not directly in front of it.

Summary

Adding an Arduino to a Raspberry Pi provides you with much broader possibilities. You'll be able to add a lot more sensors and LEDs than you're able to with Pi by itself. Among the benefits are an increased number of analog inputs, more PWM outputs, and many more digital outputs.

Arduino is very to program. If you're already familiar with C or C++, writing for the Arduino should be very familiar. However, it's very important to remember the differences between Arduino and Python. Python does not use a character at the end of a line, but Arduino ends each line with a semicolon. There is a little bit more syntax involved with writing conditionals and loops. And code blocks are contained in curly braces. Indentation is not important in Arduino, but Python will not compile if your indentation is off.

Despite these differences, there are some things Arduino makes easier. Serial communication does not take as much to set up and the serial commands are part of the core Arduino library. In Python, you have to import the serial library. Both make writing to the serial port fairly simple. Python, however, requires encoding and decoding to utf-8 to be useful. Also, Arduino makes parsing numbers in a line from the serial stream easy with the parseInt() method. Getting a number out of a string in Python requires a little gentle manipulation.

As you're working with Arduino, don't forget the community support is superb. There is very little that others have not already done and documented. Also remember that you have a great resource right in the IDE in the form of example code. Take advantage of that. And as you add more libraries for more devices, you find more example sketches to help you.

CHAPTER 6

Driving Motors

In Chapter 4, we used the Raspberry Pi's GPIO pins to control an LED and to receive information from an ultrasonic sensor. In Chapter 5, we looked at the Arduino and discussed why it is a better option for general GPIO functions. We connected the ultrasonic rangefinder and an LED to the Arduino and learned how to pass data between the two boards.

But that doesn't mean we're done with the Raspberry Pi's GPIO header. In this chapter, we'll use the GPIO pins to connect to a board called a *motor driver*, which is designed to interact with DC motors and steppers. I'll cover some of the different types of motors, and discuss what a motor driver is and why it's important in what we do.

We will connect DC motors to the motor controller and write a small program to make them turn. As part of the sample program, we'll look at how to control the speed and direction of the motors. We will also look at some of the properties of the specific motor controller selected for the workshop.

You may choose not to go with the suggested motor controller, so we'll also look at a common alternative: the L298N motor driver. The driver board, which is available from many manufacturers, is designed to connect to the L298N H-bridge controller chip at its heart. But because these boards rely on PWM signals for setting speed, we'll have to connect it through the Arduino. I'll go over all of that toward the end of the chapter.

© Jeff Cicolani 2018
J. Cicolani, *Beginning Robotics with Raspberry Pi and Arduino*,
https://doi.org/10.1007/978-1-4842-3462-4_6

By the end of this workshop, you will have the final component needed to start building robots: motion. In Chapter 7, we'll bring everything together with the chassis kit to get your robot moving.

Motors & Drivers

Before moving on to the motor controllers, let's take a moment to look at what we are controlling. The drivers we use are designed for a simple DC motor, although it could also be used to drive steppers. Let's take a look at drivers and motors in this section.

Types of Motors

Motors convert electrical energy into rotational energy. They come in many different types, and they power virtually everything that moves. The most common type of motor is the simple DC motor, which is even used in many of the other types of motors. For example, a servomotor is a device that incorporates a DC motor with a potentiometer, or other feedback device, and gearing to control precise motion, be it angular or directional. Other types of motors include the stepper, which uses electrical impulses to control very precise movement, and coreless motors, which rearrange the typical parts of a DC motor to improve efficiency.

DC Motors

DC motors consist of a series of coils within a magnetic field. When an electrical charge is placed on the coils, it causes the coils to spin on their shared axis. Simple motors have the coils arranged and attached around a central shaft. As the shaft and coils spin, electrical connectivity is maintained with brushes that make contact with the shaft. The shaft, in turn, protrudes from the assembly to use the rotational force to perform work. Figure 6-1 shows a typical DC motor.

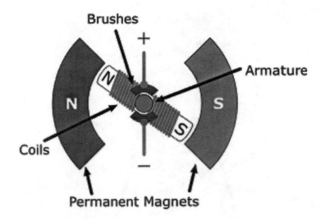

Figure 6-1. *DC motor operation*

You usually find these motors attached to gearboxes, belts, or chains that serve to amplify the torque of the motor at the cost of rotational speed. This is done because a bare DC motor can produce a lot of speed, but raw speed is rarely useful.

The motors that we are using are of this type. They are simple DC motors attached to gear boxes.

Brushless Motors

Another type of motor moves the mechanical connection to the magnets. The coils remain static. When an electrical charge is applied, the magnets spin around the coils on a common axis (see Figure 6-2). This eliminates the need for brushes, so they are called *brushless motors.*

In the hobby world, brushless motors are most commonly associated with multirotor aircraft. They are also used extensively in other areas where high speed and efficiency are required, such as in CNC (computer numerical controlled) spindles. You are probably familiar with Dremel tools or routers; both of these devices are types of spindles and use brushless motors.

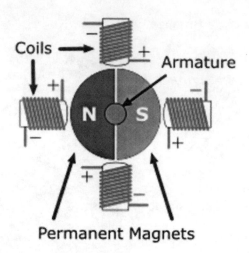

Figure 6-2. *Brushless motor operation*

Stepper Motors

All the motors that I discussed so far have one or more coils working off a single electrical charge. That charge can be positive or negative, changing the direction of the motor.

Stepper motors are different. Steppers use multiple coils with distinct charges (see Figure 6-3), which breaks a full rotation into multiple steps. By manipulating these charges, we can cause the motor to move to and hold position at one of the steps. This makes these motors extremely useful for finite control in applications such as CNC machines, 3D printers, and robotics.

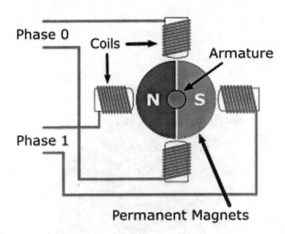

Figure 6-3. Stepper motor operation

Servos

A *servo* is a motor that moves to a specific angle and holds that position. They generally have a maximum rotation of 45 to 90 degrees in either direction. They do this by connecting a potentiometer to the final output gear. The potentiometer provides feedback to the internal control board. When the servo receives a signal, usually in the form of PWM, the motor rotates until the potentiometer and the signal balance.

Figure 6-4 shows a typical hobby servo.

Figure 6-4. *Common servomotor*

Servos with the limiters and potentiometers removed are called *continuous rotation servos*. They are used in applications where torque is required. Many robots are driven by continuous rotation servos.

This is an example where one hobby greatly benefited another. The common hobby servo was originally used for hobby RC aircraft. Since most hobbyists could not afford expensive devices to control their crafts, they figured out how to bring the price down significantly. This, of course, helps us hobby roboticists.

Motor Properties

There are a few things to keep in mind about motors in our projects. The most important is the motor's electrical properties—specifically, voltage and current.

Voltage

You're already somewhat familiar with voltage, which is a measure of the electricity needed to operate a device. The Pi is powered by 5 volts but runs on 3.3 volts. The Arduino runs on 5 volts, supplied by the USB port of the Pi. The motors we are using run on 6 volts. It is important to keep these voltages straight. If you were to put 5 volts on a device that runs on 3.3 volts, you could damage your device.

There are devices specifically designed to help manage the voltages in your project. Voltage regulators (step up or step down) maintain a constant voltage. The common 7805 5V regulator takes 6 to 12 volts and converts it to 5 volts. The excess energy is dissipated as heat, and they can get quite hot.

Voltage regulators are great for voltage supplies, but are of little use for translating 5 volts and 3.3 volts in devices. For this, we use a logic level converter, which require a reference voltage from both devices, but safely translates the voltage between devices.

So, now you are aware of the differences in the voltage needs of your devices. Next, we look at amperage.

Amperage

Amperage is a measure of current, or the electrical pressure that our devices require to operate. The most common analogy is water through a pipe, where voltage is the size of the pipe and amperage is the amount of water flowing through it. I actually like to change the analogy to use rubber tubing. If you try to push too much water through a rubber tube, bad things happen.

In the electronics world, this is frequently measured in the smaller unit of milliamps, usually noted as mA. For instance, the USB port of most devices is limited to 800mA of power. This happens to be the same amount of power used by the motors we selected; however, it does not take power spikes into account.

Voltage on a device is somewhat passive. The device uses the voltage that you provide it, never trying to draw more. Amperage is quite the opposite. A device is hungry for amperage and continues to draw what it needs until it is satisfied to do its work, or exceeds the available supply.

Components and devices have a certain amount of power that they need to work. They also have a maximum amount of power that they can withstand. Since extra electrical power is converted to heat, if you exceed the maximum tolerable amperage of a device, it gets hot and dies. Sometimes spectacularly.

The moral of the story is to "always pay attention to the current you are drawing." And this does not only apply to motors. LEDs are notorious for drawing a lot of current.

Motors and Amps

Motors are notoriously power-hungry devices. They are constantly trying to fulfil their purpose: to spin. When there is no load, weight, or resistance on a motor, it spins happily at its minimum current draw. Start to add resistance, however, and the motor draws more and more current until it reaches the maximum it can draw, which is called the *stall current*. The stall current is essentially the amperage of a motor when the shaft is physically restrained from moving.

When a motor starts, rapidly changes direction, or encounters too much resistance to spin, the power that it consumes increases drastically. If this sudden draw is too much for the supply, something is damaged. Let's take an 800mA source, such as a USB jack; if the motor suddenly draws 1 amp or greater, the USB jack will probably be damaged.

Motor Drivers

Most microcontrollers, microprocessors, and electronics can only handle a small amount of current. If one pulls too much current, it starts to burn out. Because motors usually easily exceed this maximum current, you generally don't want to connect a motor of any significant size directly to your processor. So, we will use a device called a *motor driver* or a *motor controller*.

A motor controller is designed for this specific purpose. It uses the low power signal from your microcontroller to control a much larger current and/or voltage. In our case, we are using a motor controller to control 6 volts with 3.3 volts from the GPIO pins. We are doing this through a series of components that have a much larger 1.2A (1,200mA) current tolerance and can handle brief spikes up to 3.0A (3,000mA) .

Working with Motor Controllers

Let's look two motor controllers. The first is the DC & Stepper Motor HAT by Adafruit. This controller board is designed specifically to mount onto the Raspberry Pi. The combination of utility and convenience makes it my preferred choice for projects like ours.

The other motor controller is the L298N, which is an H-bridge IC. Although the L298N is actually a discreet component—a chip, there are many manufacturers that have built onto a convenient breakout board. This type of board is typically being referred to when someone mentions an L298N motor controller. The one used in this book is a generic version that I found on Amazon for $5. Some of my friends said that I paid too much for it.

Adafruit DC & Stepper Motor HAT

The motor driver in this project is one from Adafruit available at `www.adafruit.com/products/2348`. Information on how to use it is at `https://learn.adafruit.com/adafruit-dc-and-stepper-motor-hat-for-raspberry-pi`. In fact, much of what we'll be going over came from this Adafruit website.

There are several reasons why this device was selected for our robot; not the least of which is that is mounts directly to the Raspberry Pi, thus limiting the area needed for mounting electronics on the robot. As you'll quickly learn, mounting space is at a premium on most robots; especially if you're trying to keep it rather compact. The following are some of the other reasons to use this board:

- It can control up to four DC motors or two stepper motors.

- Communication is handled via the I2C serial channel, which allows multiple devices to be stacked (this is why we used the longer pins on the header).

- Because it is using I²C, it has its own dedicated PWM module for controlling the motors, so we don't have to rely on the PWM on the Pi proper.

- It has four H-Bridge motor control circuits with 1.2A current, 3.0A peak current, with thermal shutdown, and internal protection diodes to protect your board.

- There are four bidirectional motor controls with 8-bit speed control (0 to 255).

- There is an easy connection with the use of terminal blocks.

- There are ready-made Python libraries.

Some Assembly Required

The board comes in a kit and requires soldering. If you haven't already done so, you need to assemble it before proceeding with the project. Remember, we specified longer pins for the header, so don't use the one that came with the kit.

It's time for soldering practice.

There are a lot of small pins (40 of them) that need to be soldered. If you're not familiar with soldering, you need to take a moment to learn how. Although it is remarkably easy, soldering instruction is beyond the scope of this book. There are many helpful videos available on the Internet. I also strongly suggest that you find your local makerspace. There is certainly someone there who can give you a quick lesson. Figure 6-5 shows my simple soldering setup.

Figure 6-5. *Preparing to assemble the motor HAT*

Assembling the Motor HAT is very easy, although there is soldering involved. You can find detailed instructions for assembly on the Adafruit website at `https://learn.adafruit.com/adafruit-dc-and-stepper-motor-hat-for-raspberry-pi/assembly`.

For this exercise, you need a soldering iron and solder. I recommend having some flux handy, as well as something to keep the soldering tip clean. Back in school, we used a wet sponge to clean the tip, but there are better things made for the job now. Your Raspberry Pi will help, too.

1. Mount the extended header onto the Raspberry Pi's 40-pin header (see Figure 6-6). This helps stabilize things as you solder.

Figure 6-6. *Extended stacking header on the Pi's 40-pin GPIO*

2. Mount the Motor HAT circuit board onto the headers (see Figure 6-7). To help hold the board at a better angle for soldering, you may want to put something to support the other side. One of the terminal blocks works well for this.

Figure 6-7. *Circuit board mounted on the header*

3. Solder the first pin.

4. Once the first pin is soldered, heat it up again and adjust the board so that it sits properly (see Figure 6-8). When the solder for the pin cools, it will hold the board at the right angle while you solder the rest of the pins. If you supported the board with a terminal block or something else so that the board is sitting straight, you may be able to skip this step.

Figure 6-8. *Adjusting the placement and angle of the board*

5.   Solder the rest of the first row (see Figure 6-9).
     You want a nice, clean, shiny joint.

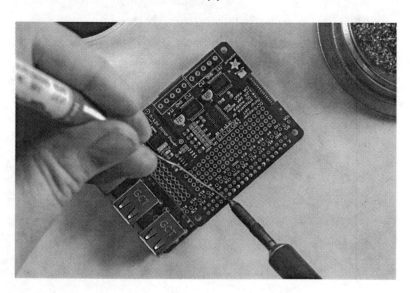

Figure 6-9. *Solder the first row of pins*

6. Rotate the board 180 degrees and solder the second
    row (see Figure 6-10).

Figure 6-10.   *Rotate the Pi and solder the remaining pins*

7. Remove the HAT from the Pi.

8. Mount the screw terminals onto the board
    (see Figure 6-11).

Figure 6-11. *Adding the terminal blocks to the circuit board*

9. Use tape to hold the terminals in place while you flip the board over (see Figure 6-12).

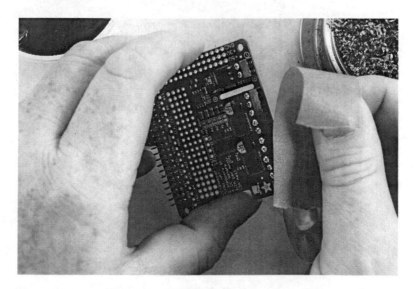

Figure 6-12. *Tape helps hold the terminal blocks on the board while you turn it over to solder them into place*

10.   Solder the terminals in place (see Figure 6-13).

Figure 6-13. *Soldering the terminal pins*

Once you've removed the tape, you are done. The Motor HAT is ready for use. Mount the HAT onto the Pi. You want to support the side with the terminals so that it doesn't short across the HDMI housing (see Figure 6-14).

Figure 6-14. *The completed board mounted on the Raspberry Pi. The orange support piece is 3D printed.*

Hooking up the Motor Controller

Connecting the Motor HAT is pretty straightforward. Simply mount the board on the GPIO headers of the Pi. There are a couple of things to note, however. First, be careful not to bend any of the pins on either the Raspberry Pi or the HAT. It is remarkably easy to do. The header pins on the Motor HAT are particularly susceptible to bending.

You also want to be careful not to short the terminal blocks. You'll notice that when mounted, the solder joints are precariously close to the metal housing of the HDMI connection (see Figure 6-15). There are two easy solutions for this. The first fix (and this is what we'll do in the workshop until you can apply the second solution) is to simply place a piece of electrical tape over the metal housings of the micro USB and HDMI connectors of the Pi. The second fix (recommended) is to get some offsets to support that side of the HAT. Spacers and screws will also do the job. The point is that you don't want the board to sag and make contact with the housing, which would probably result in a brief light show and the destruction of both the Motor HAT and the Pi.

Figure 6-15. *Adafruit Motor HAT mounted on a Raspberry Pi*

Once the board is mounted, and safely insulated from shorting, it's time to connect the motors. For the first tutorial, we're only going to use one motor. The second piece of code controls two, so we might as well get them connected now.

But before we can do that, we have to prep our motors. Now, if your motors came with the leads attached, then you're ahead of the game. If not, you'll need to solder leads to your motor, as shown in Figure 6-16. I tend to use black and red wires of appropriate size for the motors in question. I also like to make sure that the leads on each of the motors match (the black wire goes to the same pole on each of the motors, and the red to the same poles on each motor). This way I don't have to second-guess how things are connected later.

Figure 6-16. *Leads soldered to motor terminals*

In this case, I'm using 26AWG-stranded wire. There are generally two types of lead wire: stranded and solid. Solid is more rigid and excellent for jumpers or situations where there isn't going to be a lot of moment. Stranded wire consists of multiple thinner wires housed in a single sheathing. It is more flexible and ideal for applications where there will likely be movement. Stranded wire is a little harder to work with and the ends going into the terminal blocks should be tinned, or coated in solder (see Figure 6-17). This makes that end rigid, and it connects better in the terminal block.

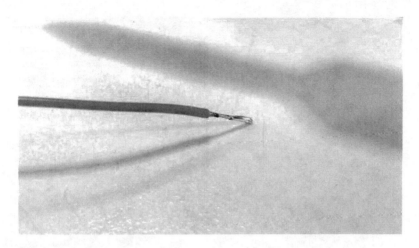

Figure 6-17. *Tinned lead*

The next steps connect the motors to the terminal block.

1. Make sure that the terminal blocks are open with the screw inside the block all the way to the top. Be sure not to remove the screw. You'll need to use a pretty fine Phillips head screwdriver.

2. Insert one of the tinned leads into the hole on the side of the terminal block marked M1 (see Figure 6-18). It doesn't matter, which wire goes to which port, as long as both wires go to different ports for the same driver (in this case, M1).

3. Tighten the screw corresponding to the hole you inserted the wire into.

4. Repeat the procedure for the second lead from the motor.

Figure 6-18. *Motor connected to the Motor HAT*

At this point, if you are so inclined, you can connect the second motor as well. I tend to reverse the order of the leads since they are destined for opposite sides of the robot. You want a *forward* command to turn the left motor in one direction and the right motor in the other direction. If they both turn in the same direction electrically, then the robot just spins in place.

You'll repeat the procedure for the four-AA battery pack to the power terminals. Make sure that the red lead goes to the positive (+) side and the black goes to the negative (–) side (see Figure 6-19).

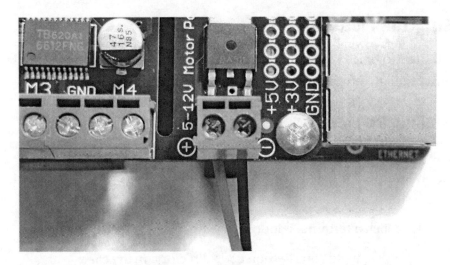

Figure 6-19. *External battery pack connected to the Motor HAT*

Your board and motors should look similar to Figure 6-20. With both motors and the battery pack connected, you are ready to start coding!

Figure 6-20. *Completed connections to the Motor HAT*

Using the Motor HAT

With the Motor HAT mounted, and your motors and motor power supply connected, it's time to boot up the Pi and log on.

Installing the Library

Once you've started up and connected to your Pi, you need to install the Python libraries for the Motor HAT. These are available from the Adafruit GitHub site.

1. Open a terminal window.

2. Navigate to your Python code directory. In my case, it is TRG-RasPi_Robot.

3. Enter the following:

   ```
   git clone https://github.com/adafruit/Adafruit-Motor-
   HAT-Python-Library.git
   cd Adafruit-Motor-HAT-Python-Library
   ```

4. Install the Python development libraries.

   ```
   sudo apt-get install python-dev
   ```

5. Install the Motor HAT libraries.

   ```
   sudo python setup.py install
   ```

At this point, your Pi is updated with the necessary libraries, and it's time to get started with the code.

The Code

Before we start coding, there is one quick but important note. Previously, we used Python 3 for just about everything. For this workshop, we will use Python 2.7. Why? Well, the default libraries provided by Adafruit are in

Python 2.7. There may be Python 3.x libraries, but we are going with the default libraries for this workshop.

As you've discovered in earlier workshops, anytime that you use the GPIO pins, you need to run your code as a super user (sudo). There are a few ways to do it. One way is to save your Python code, make the file executable, and then run the program with sudo. This is the proper way for code that you'll run in the future. For the workshop, we'll take a shortcut. We'll launch the IDLE IDE using sudo from the command line, which makes any programs run from that instance of IDLE run with sudo.

Turning a Single Motor

1. Open a terminal window. You can use the same one used for the installation; but as long as IDLE is open, this terminal window is locked.

2. Type **sudo idle**.

3. In the IDLE IDE, create a new file and save it as motors.py.

4. Enter the following code:

```
from Adafruit_MotorHAT import Adafruit_MotorHAT as amhat
from Adafruit_MotorHAT import Adafruit_DCMotor as adcm

import time

# create a motor object
mh = amhat(addr=0x60)
myMotor = mh.getMotor(1)

# set start speed
myMotor.setSpeed(150)
```

```
while True:
    # set direction
    myMotor.run(amhat.FORWARD)

    # wait 1 second
    time.sleep(1)

    # stop motor
    myMotor.run(amhat.RELEASE)

    # wait 1 second
    time.sleep(1)
```

5. Save the file.

6. Press F5 to run the program.

Let's go through the code.

We start by importing the objects we need from the Adafruit_
MotorHAT library and assign them aliases so that we don't have to write
the whole name each time we use them. We also import the time library
for our delays later in the code.

```
from Adafruit_MotorHAT import Adafruit_MotorHAT as amhat
from Adafruit_MotorHAT import Adafruit_DCMotor as adcm

import time
```

Next, we create an instance of the motor object. To do this, we tell Python
that we are using the Motor HAT located at the default I2C address, 0x60.
We then create a motor object for the motor attached to M1, or motor 1.
This lets us access the motor's methods and properties.

```
mh = amhat(addr=0x60)
myMotor = mh.getMotor(1)
```

Before we turn on the motors, for this program, we set the start speed at a little over half speed.

```
myMotor.setSpeed(150)
```

Now we wrap the remainder of the motor drive code in a while loop. As long as the True value is true, this code will keep executing.

```
while True:
```

The code to drive the motor is very simple. We drive the motor forward for one second, and then stop the motor for one second. The program keeps doing this.

```
# set direction
myMotor.run(amhat.FORWARD)

# wait 1 second
time.sleep(1)

# stop motor
myMotor.run(amhat.RELEASE)

# wait 1 second
time.sleep(1)
```

Hit Ctrl-C on the keyboard.

Note that the program ended, but the motor continues to turn. That's because the Motor HAT is freely running. This means that the controller continues with the last command received from the Pi. If we don't tell it to stop, it won't.

Now we are going to do something interesting; something we haven't done before. We'll wrap the motor drive code into a try/except block. It is a piece of code that allows us to capture any errors that occur, and then gracefully handles them.

In this particular case, we are going to use the `try/except` block to capture the `KeyboardInterrupt` event. This event is triggered when we use Ctrl-C to exit a program.

1. Change the code for the `while` loop to read as follows:

```
try:
    while True:
        # set direction
        myMotor.run(amhat.FORWARD)

        # wait 1 second
        time.sleep(1)

        # stop motor
        myMotor.run(amhat.RELEASE)

        # wait 1 second
        time.sleep(1)

except KeyboardInterrupt:
    myMotor.run(amhat.RELEASE)
```

2. Run the program.

3. Let it run for a moment, and then press Ctrl-C.

The motor will now stop when the program exits.

Python captures the `KeyboardInterrupt` event and executes that last line of code before exiting. The code releases the motor, and simply turns it off.

Turning Two Motors

Turning a single motor is great and dandy, but our robot is going to have two motors, and we want them to operate independently. We also want them to be able to change speed and direction.

To operate multiple motors, you simply need to create a different instance of the motor object for each motor. Assuming that you connected both of your motors earlier, we are creating two motors and giving commands to each. We are also changing both the speed and direction of the motors.

1. Create a new Python file from IDLE.

2. Save the file as two_motors.py.

3. Enter the following code:

```python
from Adafruit_MotorHAT import Adafruit_MotorHAT as
amhat, Adafruit_DCMotor as adcm

import time

# create 2 motor objects
mh = amhat(addr=0x60)

motor1 = mh.getMotor(1)
motor2 = mh.getMotor(2)

# set start speed
motor1.setSpeed(0)
motor2.setSpeed(0)

# direction variable
direction = 0

# wrap actions in try loop
try:
    while True:
        # if direction = 1 then motor1 forward and
        motor2 backward
        # else motor1 backward and motor2 forward
```

```
            if direction == 0:
                motor1.run(amhat.FORWARD)
                motor2.run(amhat.BACKWARD)
            else:
                motor1.run(amhat.BACKWARD)
                motor2.run(amhat.FORWARD)

            # ramp up the speed from 1 to 255
            for i in range(255):
                j = 255-i

                motor1.setSpeed(i)
                motor2.setSpeed(j)

                time.sleep(0.01)

            # ramp down the speed from 255 to 1
            for i in reversed(range(255)):
                j = 255-i

                motor1.setSpeed(i)
                motor2.setSpeed(j)

                time.sleep(0.01)

            # wait half a second
            time.sleep(0.5)

            # change directions
            if direction == 0:
                direction = 1
            else:
                direction = 0
```

```
# kill motors and exit program on ctrl-c
except KeyboardInterrupt:
    motor1.run(amhat.RELEASE)
    motor2.run(amhat.RELEASE)
```

4. Save the file.

5. Press F5 to run the program.

For the most part, the code is the same. We added a few for loops to count up to 255 and back down again. We created two variables to hold this value; the second one inverts the value by subtracting it from 255. We also have a variable to track the direction that the motors are turning in. Once both motors have sped up and down again, we change direction and do it again. We use the same exit code as we did before.

L298N Generic Motor Driver

The L298N is a common H-bridge motor controller chip. Several manufacturers have mounted the chip on a board and added all the necessary support electronics. The end result is a popular, generic motor controller.

H-bridge Motor Controller

The H-bridge motor controller is the most common motor controller that you will encounter. It gets its name from the distinctive H shape seen in the schematic. An H-bridge essentially consists of four gates that control current flow through the motor. Depending on how the gates are opened and closed, you can control the direction in which the motor spins.

On the L298N, there are two enable pins (one for each motor) and four input pins. The in1 and in2 pins control motor 1, while in3 and in4 control motor 2. Figure 6-21 shows how the gates are arranged; in1 controls S1 and

S4, and in2 controls S3 and S2. When in1 or in2 are high, their respective gates are closed. When they are low, the gates open.

When in1 is high and in2 is low, the current flows so that the motor spins clockwise. If in1 is low and in2 is high, the motor spins counter-clockwise. If both pins are high, the motor does not spin, essentially putting on a brake. If both pins are low, no current is flowing through the motor and it is spinning freely.

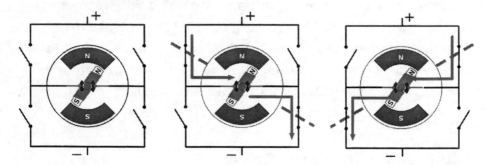

Figure 6-21. *H-bridge motor controller operation*

That leaves the enable pins, enA and enB, which are used for setting the speeds of the motors. This is why we use PWM on these pins. PWM allows us to vary the speed of each motor. If we used a standard digital pin, we could start and stop the motor, but it would be either full power or no power. PWM allows us to have more control over our motors.

Using the L298N

There are a few ways to use the L298N; each has its benefits and faults. One method is to connect the pins to the Raspberry Pi, which has the virtue of being directly controlled by the Pi. The drawbacks are that you may have to use a logic level converter since the Pi's pins are 3.3 volts and the controller is 5 volts. Also, you lose the ability to control the speed. Speed control requires PWM, and as I discussed in earlier chapters, that is one area where the Pi is wanting.

My preferred method for connecting to the L298N is through the Arduino. In this way, you have speed control through PWM. Also, since the Arduino and the controller are both 5 volts, there is no need to use a logic level converter. Of course, the drawback here is that you have to pass the motor instructions via serial to the Arduino.

Arduino Code

For this exercise, the Arduino is simply going to act as a pass-through for the motor controller. We will read the instructions from the serial stream and pass those values on to the motor controller. The Arduino will perform no logic. If you implement this in a real-world scenario, you may want the sensors to act as an interrupt. By allowing the sensors to interrupt the normal operation, you can build some safeties into the project.

1. Open a new sketch in the Arduino IDE.

2. Save the sketch as L298N_passthrough.

3. Enter the following code:

```
int enA = 9;
int in1 = 8;
int in2 = 7;
int in3 = 5;
int in4 = 4;
int enB = 3;

int enAVal, in1Val, in2Val, in3Val, in4Val, enBVal;

void setup() {
  // put your setup code here, to run once:
  Serial.begin(9600);

  pinMode(enA, OUTPUT);
  pinMode(in1, OUTPUT);
  pinMode(in2, OUTPUT);
```

```
      pinMode(in3, OUTPUT);
      pinMode(in4, OUTPUT);
      pinMode(enB, OUTPUT);
  }

  void loop() {
    // Only work if there is data in the serial buffer
    while(Serial.available() > 0){

      // Read the ints from the serial port
      enAVal = Serial.parseInt();
      in1Val = Serial.parseInt();
      in2Val = Serial.parseInt();
      // Only read the next three if there is data
      if(Serial.available() > 0){
        in3Val = Serial.parseInt();
        in4Val = Serial.parseInt();
        enBVal = Serial.parseInt();
      }

      // Write the values to the L298N
      analogWrite(enA, enAVal);
      digitalWrite(in1, in1Val);
      digitalWrite(in2, in2Val);
      digitalWrite(in3, in3Val);
      digitalWrite(in4, in4Val);
      analogWrite(enB, enBVal);

      // Purge any remaining data because we don't need it
      while(Serial.available() > 0){
        char x = Serial.read();
      }
    }
  }
```

4.   Save the sketch and upload it to the Arduino.

You won't see anything happening on the Arduino. What we've done is load the Arduino with code that simply reads the serial port and passes the values read to the L298N.

We did a few things in this code that you want to take note of.

```
if(Serial.available() > 2){
```

The first thing to note is the `if` statement after we read in the value for `in2Val`. This code is used in both of the upcoming exercises. The first exercise will only pass three values. The second will pass six values. We only read the second three values if they exist; otherwise, we'll get an error. To assure that we avoid the error, we only want to read the next three values if there are three or more values to read.

```
while(Serial.available() > 0){
  char x = Serial.read();
}
```

At the end of the sketch, we added a small `while` loop. If we have anything left in the serial buffer after reading all six values, we need to clear it out so that there is no straggling data in the buffer for the next cycle. This block simply reads all the remaining bytes and removes them from the buffer.

Hooking up the L298N

Hooking up the motor controller is a little more complicated than just plugging it into the header. We'll connect through the Arduino to take advantage of the PWM pins. As with the Motor HAT, we'll provide the motor controller with external power from the four AAA battery pack. This provides the 6 volts that the motors want, without frying the Arduino.

Turning One Motor

In the first exercise with L298N, you learn how to turn a single motor. We set the motor's speed and direction, change the direction, and vary the speed. Figure 6-22 shows the circuit for this exercise.

1. Connect enA on the motor controller to pin 9 on the Arduino. You may need to remove a jumper.

2. Connect in1 to pin 8.

3. Connect in2 to pin 7.

4. Connect a ground pin on the Arduino to the ground post on the screw terminal. This is likely the middle post.

5. Connect a motor to the motor controller by connecting one lead to out1 and the other to out2.

    At the moment, it doesn't matter which lead goes to which output post.

6. Connect the black lead from the battery pack to the ground terminal on the L298N.

7. Connect the red lead from the battery pack to the positive terminal. It is usually labeled + or VCC.

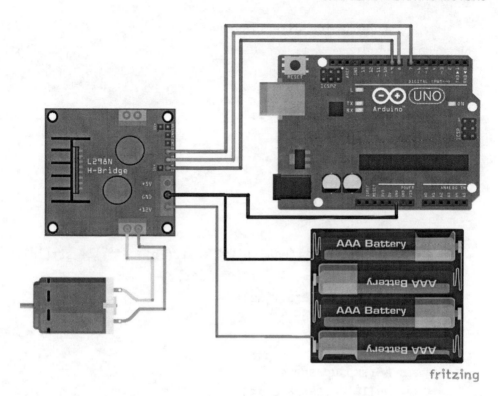

Figure 6-22. *L298N single motor wiring*

8. Open a new file in IDLE.

9. Save the file as L298N_1_motor_example.py.

10. Enter the following code:

```
import serial
import time

directon = 1

ser = serial.Serial("/dev/ttyACM0",9600,timeout=1)

def driveMotor(int speed, int drct):
    enA = speed
```

223

```
            # determine direction
            if drct == 1:
                in1 = 1
                in2 = 0
            else if drct == -1:
                in1 = 0
                in2 = 1
            else:
                in1 = 0
                in2 = 0

            valList = str(enA) + ',' + str(in1) + ',' + str(in2)
            serString = ','.join(valList)
            ser.write(serString)
            time.sleep(0.1)

    while 1:
        # ramp up speed
        while motSpeed < 256:
            driveMotor(motSpeed, direction)
            motSpeed = motSpeed + 1

        # ramp down speed
        while motSpeed > 0:
            driveMotor(motSpeed, direction)
            motSpeed = motSpeed - 1

        # reverse direction
        direction = -direction
```

11. Save and run the file

The motor should begin spinning, getting faster until it reaches its top speed. At that time, it slows to a stop, reverses direction, and repeats. This continues until you press Ctrl-C to stop the program.

Turning Two Motors

Next, we spin two motors. The setup and code are very similar to what we just did, with an additional motor. You should already have the first motor connected. If not, complete steps 1 through 7 from the previous exercise. Let's pick up with the addition of the second motor (see Figure 6-23).

1. Connect a lead from pin 5 on the Arduino to in3 on the motor controller.

2. Connect a lead from pin 4 to in4.

3. Connect a lead from pin 3 to enB.

4. Connect the leads from the second motor to the out2 terminals. Again, it matters very little in this exercise which lead goes to which terminal. Later, when you are mounting the motors onto the robot, you want to make sure that the motors are connected so that they turn opposite to each other. For now, however, we only care that they actually turn.

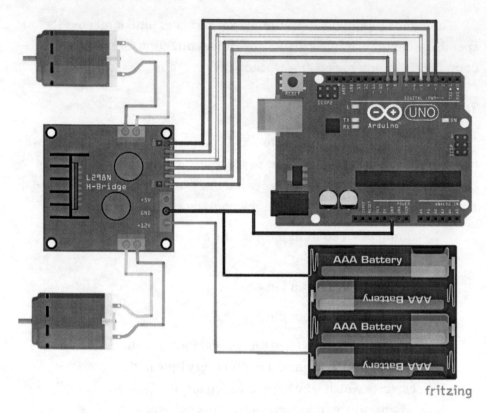

fritzing

Figure 6-23. *L298N two motor wiring*

5. Open a new file in IDLE.

6. Save the file as L298N_2_motor_example.py.

7. Enter the following code:

```
import serial
import time

directon = 1

ser = serial.Serial("/dev/ttyACM0",9600,timeout=1)

def driveMotor(int motor, int speed, int drct):
    enA = speed
```

```python
    # determine direction
    if drct == 1:
        in1 = 1
        in2 = 0
        in3 = 1
        in4 = 0
    else if drct == -1:
        in1 = 0
        in2 = 1
        in3 = 0
        in4 = 1
    else:
        in1 = 0
        in2 = 0
        in3 = 0
        in4 = 0

    valList = str(enA) + ',' + str(in1) + ',' + str(in2) +
        ',' + str(in3) + ',' + str(in4) + ',' + str(enB)
    serString = ','.join(valList)
    ser.write(serString)
    time.sleep(0.1)

while 1:
    # ramp up speed
    while motSpeed < 256:
        driveMotor(motSpeed, direction)
        motSpeed = motSpeed + 1

    # ramp down speed
    while motSpeed > 0:
        driveMotor(motSpeed, direction)
        motSpeed = motSpeed - 1
```

```
# reverse direction
direction = -direction
```

This code was not much different from the previous exercise. All that we did was add the enable and input variables for the second motor. Both motors should be spinning at the same speed. They speed up, slow down, and then reverse direction. Take a look at the code and determine how to get the motors to spin independently of each other.

Summary

In this chapter, we looked at the common types of motors: DC, coreless, stepper, and servo. We assembled the Adafruit DC & Stepper Motor HAT. (You should now be pretty comfortable with the soldering iron.) Then, you learned how to connect your motors to it and made them spin.

We also looked at a common, generic motor controller. The L298N works a little differently in that the direction is set by altering the state of two pins. We connected the L298N through the Arduino to take advantage of the PWM pins to control the speed of the motors, as well as the direction. We could have just as easily connected the enable pins to digital out pins on the Raspberry Pi GPIO header. However, having discrete control of the motors' speed is important. In an upcoming chapter, you see why this is important.

At this point, you have all the information that you need to build a simple little robot. You've learned about programming in both Python and Arduino. You've worked with sensors to allow your robot to detect its surroundings. And finally, you got your motors to spin, so you have motion. Logic, sensing, and movement are the essence of every robot. Everything else is a more advanced version of these elements.

Now that you know everything you need to about robots, we're going to assemble the chassis kit and build a robot. After that, we jump into making our robot more capable and smarter. We starting with IR sensors, move on to control algorithms, and then give the robot eyes. Well, an eye.

CHAPTER 7

Assembling the Robot

In the last chapter, we built the Adafruit Motor HAT, an electronic device that allows you to control up to four DC motors with your Raspberry Pi. We also looked at a generic motor controller that we ran through the Arduino board. Now that you know how to get your robot to move, let's start building it.

In this chapter, we will build our robot. Along the way, I'll give some tips and pointers I've picked up in my builds. There are a lot of little things to consider when assembling a robot. You'll encounter some odd scenarios that you hadn't considered. The most overlooked is wiring and wire management. Things like order of operations and component placement are very important. Decisions made early in a build can cause complications later. Being mindful of these things can help keep you from having to disassemble your robot to correct an error that you made early on.

The build is broken into four separate exercises. We'll start by building the Whippersnapper chassis kit. Then we'll mount the electronics, which is followed by the wiring. Finally, we'll look at mounting the ultrasonic sensors. In each exercise, I'll point out some of the things to consider when working on your own build.

© Jeff Cicolani 2018
J. Cicolani, *Beginning Robotics with Raspberry Pi and Arduino*,
https://doi.org/10.1007/978-1-4842-3462-4_7

Assembling the Chassis

For this build, I chose to use a commercially available kit. The nice thing about kits is that a good kit has everything you need to get started. There are many options at many different price points and from many different manufacturers. Many of the low-cost kits, generally found online from foreign sellers, are less complete than others. Often, these are kits for popular devices but are assembled with little thought on how the parts go together. So, if you're going to buy a kit, make sure that it's got all the hardware and that the parts are designed to work together.

Choosing a Material

The materials are another thing to consider when selecting a chassis. A metal chassis is good. It tends to be more costly than a plastic chassis, but it also tends to be a lot more durable. In terms of plastic kits, remember that not all plastics are the same.

Acrylic is an inexpensive and convenient material to use; however, it is not the right material for most applications. Acrylic is brittle, inflexible, and scratches easily. When it breaks, it usually does so in sharp pieces. It is also wise to remember not to use acrylic in any kind of high-friction application because it tends to breakdown into course granules that amplify the friction.

If you're going to use plastics, ABS is a better material to use. Like acrylic, ABS comes in sheets and is fairly inexpensive. Unlike acrylic, it is much more durable. It doesn't crack or break as easily, and it is more scratch resistant. ABS is drillable and easier to work with than acrylic is.

Another option is polystyrene. Styrene is the material used for plastic model kits. So, if you're familiar with working with these kits, then styrene is an easy choice. It is more flexible than either acrylic or ABS. It tends to be a little more expensive than the others are, but it is easy to work with.

The Whippersnapper

The Whippersnapper is a commercial kit made with lasercut ABS sheets. It is part of the Runt Rover line from Actobotics, manufactured by ServoCity. I have worked with several kits from the Actobotics line, and I know them to be well-designed, quality products. In addition to the robot kits, they produce a broad line of parts that are designed to work together.

All of these things contributed to the selection of the Whippersnapper (see Figure 7-1) for the base of this project. It doesn't hurt that it's a good-looking chassis with space to hold all the electronics and leave some room to grow.

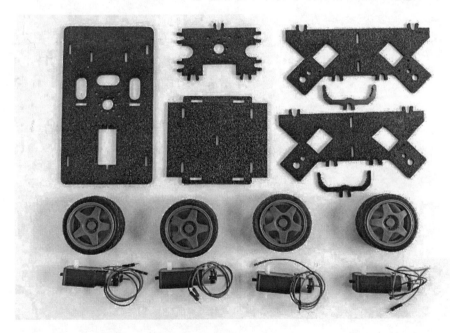

Figure 7-1. *All the Whippersnapper parts*

For the sake of clarification, the Raspberry Pi will be mounted at the back of the robot. The Arduino will be at the front. This will make the wiring a little easier.

To begin, I like to lay out the parts. This helps you make sure that everything is there and gets you familiar with all the parts. This kit snaps together. In fact, the only tools that you need are a Philips screwdriver and needle-nose pliers. When snapping the parts together, be aware that the fit is tight and that it takes some force to get everything to go together. As long as you keep the parts straight, they won't break. Keep a firm grip on the part and apply even pressure.

1. Attach the center support to one of the sides. Make sure that the course side is facing out. Take note of the tabs on the center support. The single pair of tabs attaches to the bottom plate (see Figure 7-2).

Figure 7-2. *Center support attached to an outer plate*

2. Attach the second side plate to the center support. Again, make sure that the course side is on the outside of the robot.

3. Snap the top plate to the assembly. There are six sets of tabs that snap to the top plate (see Figure 7-3).

Figure 7-3. *Top plate added*

In the next steps, we attach the motors. On one side of the motor is a small peg (see Figure 7-4), which helps align the motor and keeps it in place.

Figure 7-4. *Motor with tab*

1. Mount the motor so that the shaft goes through the lower hole and the peg goes into the second one.

2. Use two screws and nuts to hold the motor in place (see Figure 7-5). Although not included in the kit, some #4 split lock washers would be good to use here. If you don't have any, use Loctite Threadlocker Blue on the nuts. Without something to lock them into place, the nuts will rattle off.

Figure 7-5. *Mounted motor*

3. Repeat the process for each of the three remaining motors (see Figure 7-6).

Figure 7-6. *All motors mounted*

4. Flip the chassis over and attach the bottom plate.
    There are five sets of tabs holding the bottom plate
    on (see Figure 7-7).

Figure 7-7. Bottom plate added

5.   Feed the wires for each motor into the chassis
     through the hole behind the motor (see Figure 7-8).
     This bit of housekeeping keeps the wires from getting
     tangled in the wheels or caught onto something.

Figure 7-8. *Motor wires fed through the hole behind the motor*

6. Attach the electronics clips to the top plate. These clips will be used for holding the Raspberry Pi.

7. Feed the wires for the front motors through the hole in the center support plate.

The chassis is now ready to have the electronics mounted to it. Your robot chassis should look like what's shown in Figure 7-9.

Figure 7-9. *The completed Whippersnapper*

Mounting the Electronics

Next, we'll mount the electronics to the chassis. Starting with the Raspberry Pi, we'll attach each component, with the Arduino and the breadboard mounted toward the front.

During this part of the build, mounting tape and zip ties are used frequently. The placement of the boards is up to you. Some people mount some of the electronics inside the chassis. However, I've found the following arrangement to work the best for me. It allows easier access to the electronics and saves space inside for additional components.

1. Snap the Raspberry Pi into the clips on the top plate
    (see Figure 7-10). The Pi should be held firmly in
    place by the top barbs.

Figure 7-10.   *Raspberry Pi mounted in the clips*

The tabs that hold the chassis together (see Figure 7-11) make
mounting the Arduino and breadboard a challenge. This is one reason
I like to use foam mounting tape—it provides some padding. To clear the
tabs, we'll need to double up on the tape.

Figure 7-11. *Clip protruding from the top plate*

2. Stack two pieces of foam tape on top of each other and place them on the top plate. Use a second set of stacked foam tape to form a T (see Figure 7-12). This adds stability.

Figure 7-12. *Double layer of mounting tape for the breadboard*

3.   Remove the protective paper from the bottom of the
     breadboard and press the breadboard firmly into
     the T-shaped tape on the top plate (see Figure 7-13).

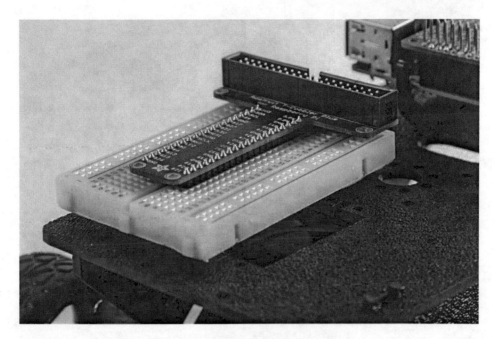

Figure 7-13. *Mounted breadboard. Note that the T-cobbler has been moved forward to allow room for the power pack.*

4. Repeat the procedure for the Arduino
    (see Figure 7-14).

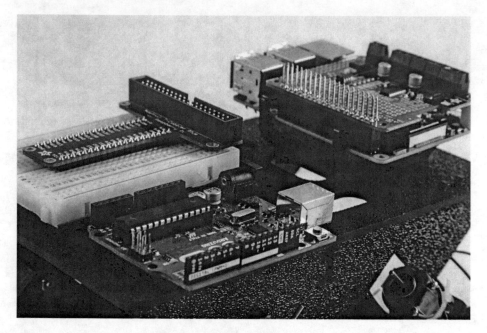

Figure 7-14. *Arduino mounted on a double layer of mounting tape*

When mounting the Arduino, remember to leave room for the USB cable. I offset the Arduino from the center so that the USB plug is clear of the Raspberry Pi (see Figure 7-15).

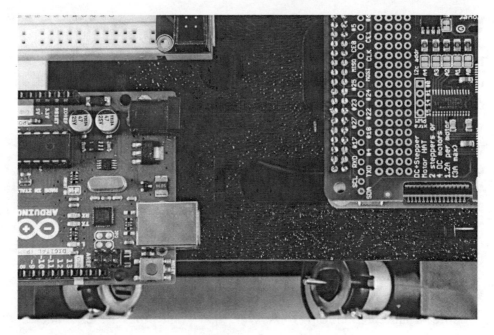

Figure 7-15. *Leaving clearance for the USB cable*

5. Mount the 4 AA battery holder inside the chassis in the back. Be sure to mount it in such a way that it allows access to the batteries and the power switch, if applicable. I used foam mounting tape to hold mine in place.

6. Find a place to securely mount the 5V power bank. I find that the space between the breadboard and the Raspberry Pi works well for the small power banks that I use. Your placement will be determined by the form factor of your power bank.

With the electronics in place, it's time to start wiring the parts together.

Wiring

It would be inappropriate to try to write this part as step-by-step instructions. How you wire your robot is entirely up to you. Each robot is different. Wiring is determined by component placement, the cables that you use, and personal preference. Instead, I'll walk you through how I wired my robot and the thought process behind my decisions, and include considerations for your project.

I prefer to keep my cables a tidy as possible. Some people put little thought into how they run the wires. I've seen some tangled messes under the covers of some robots. It's important to me to be able to access the parts easily, and this includes the wires and cables.

The USB cables for powering the Pi and connecting to the Arduino are a little longer than I prefer for most projects. There are numerous types of cables available, including those with right-angle plugs, which make cabling fairly easy. Because the cables are a little long, I use zip ties to bundle them into something smaller. The heavier cable for the Arduino is then bound to the mounting clips for the Pi. The cable from the power bank to the Pi is tucked underneath the Pi (see Figure 7-16).

Figure 7-16. *USB cables bundled for tidiness*

Next, I connect the wires from the motors to the Motor HAT. The Motor HAT has four outputs for DC motors. There are four motors. I could attach the motors in pairs to two different outputs: one for the left side and one for the right; however, the small, inexpensive motors tend not to be very consistent in speed. Even though two motors receive the same signal, there is no guarantee that they will turn at the same rate. Being able to adjust the speed of each motor independently is a nice feature that I take advantage of. So, each motor has its own output (see Figure 7-17).

Figure 7-17. *Motor and external battery pack wires connected to the Motor HAT*

I include a multiplier to the speed of each motor. With a little fine-tuning of the multiplier, I can get the motors to turn more consistently.

Once the motors are connected, I connect the power. When you connect yours, pay attention to the polarity. As a standard, red is positive and black is negative. Since my battery pack is modified, the wires are not red and black. I used a voltmeter to determine the polarity of the wires and connect them appropriately.

The last cable to connect is the ribbon cable for the T-cobbler (see Figure 7-18). There is only one way to attach the ribbon cable to the T-cobbler. A tab on the plug aligns to a gap on the plug. On the Pi, make sure that the wire with the white stripe goes to pin 1. For the Pi, this is the pin closest to the corner.

Figure 7-18. *Ribbon cable attaches the T-cobbler to the Pi. Note the white stripe.*

Mounting Sensors

This is where assembling the robot takes the most creativity. Most chassis do not come with mounting hardware for sensors. If they do, they are for specific sensors that you may not use.

There are a lot of different approaches for mounting sensors. I find simply being prepared with a number of different materials tends to work well for me.

When I was growing up, I had an Erector Set. If you're not familiar with Erector, they produce a construction toy that includes a number of metal parts: beams, brackets, screws, nuts, pulleys, belts, and so forth. I spent hours building trucks, tractors, planes, and yes, even in the 1980s, robots. Imagine my delight when looking for some generic parts for use in a project, I came across an Erector Set in my local hobby store. I was even more delighted when I discovered that one of the local big-box hardware stores sells individual parts in their miscellaneous parts bins.

Erector Sets are great sources for the small miscellaneous parts needed in many projects. In this case, I use one of the beams and a bracket to mount the ultrasonic rangefinders (see Figure 7-19).

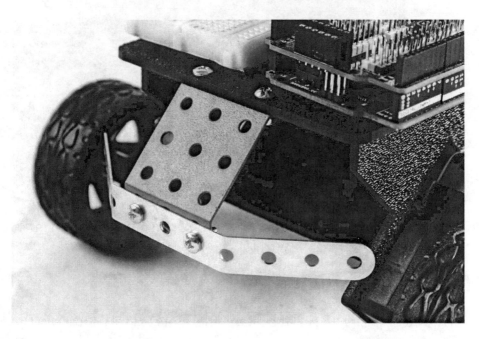

Figure 7-19. *A bracket and beam from the Erector Set. The beam is bent to provide angles for the sensors.*

With the brackets in place, I use mounting tape to attach the sensors (see Figure 7-20). In this particular case, the tape serves two purposes. First, it holds the sensors to the metal. The second purpose is insulation. The electronics on the back of the sensor are exposed; attaching them to a metal part risks causing a short. The foam mounting tape makes a good insulator.

Figure 7-20. *Ultrasonic sensors mounted*

One thing I have learned is not to trust mounting tape alone for holding sensors, especially to metal. In the past, the tape has come loose, leading to a faulty sensor. The solution is my other favorite go-to: zip ties. The tape holds the sensor in place and provides insulation; however, the zip ties add security and strength. At this point, I'm pretty sure that things aren't going anywhere.

With the sensors firmly mounted, the last thing to do is connect them to the Arduino. I use female-to-female jumpers from the sensor to the Arduino (see Figure 7-21). On the Arduino, I mount a sensor shield. The sensor shield adds a 5V and ground pin to each of the digital analog pins. Some of them even have specialty header for serial or wireless devices. I'm using a very simple one without a lot of specialty headers. The sensor shield makes it easier to attach sensors and other devices.

Figure 7-21. *Ultrasonic rangefinders secured with zip ties and wired to Arduino*

The Finished Robot

With the sensors attached, I have a complete robot. The only thing left to do is write the code to make it move. Figure 7-22 shows my completed robot.

Figure 7-22. *The finished Whippersnapper with electronics*

Making the Robot Mobile

At the moment, we have a very nice collection of parts. Without the proper software, we don't really have a robot. Next, I outline what we want the robot to do. We'll turn that into behaviors, and those, in turn, into the code needed to bring the little robot to life.

The Plan

In previous chapters, we worked with examples that illustrated various topics. Since this is our first application for the working robot, let's take a moment to outline what we want the robot to do.

This plan is based on the robot that I built earlier in this chapter. It assumes that there are three ultrasonic sensors and four motors that operate independently. The motors are controlled through the Motor HAT mounted on the Pi. The sensors are operated through the Arduino.

Sensors

As mentioned, we will operate three ultrasonic sensors. The sensors are connected to the Arduino through a sensor shield. Since we are using serial to communicate with the Pi, we cannot use pins 0 and 1. These are the pins used by the serial port. So, our first sensor, the middle, is on pins 2 and 3; the left sensor is on pins 4 and 5; and the right sensor is on pins 6 and 7.

The sensors are triggered in sequence, starting with the middle, followed by the left, and then the right. Each sensor waits until the previous one is done before triggering. The results are sent back to the Pi in half-second intervals as a string of floats representing the distance from each sensor in centimeters.

Motors

The motors are connected to the Motor HAT on the Raspberry Pi. Each motor is connected to one of the four motor channels on the controller. Motor 1, the front left motor, is connected to M1. Motor 2, the back left motor, is connected to M2. Motor 3, the front right motor, is on M3. And, motor 4, the back right motor, is on M4.

The robot drives using *differential steering*, also called *tank drive* or *skid steering*. To do this, the left motors drive together and the right ones drive together. I refer to them as *left* and *right channels*. So, the same commands are sent to M1 and M2. Likewise, M3 and M4 receive shared commands.

The code has multipliers for each motor. The multipliers are applied to each respective motor to compensate for differences in speed. The implication is that we need to allow a buffer to accommodate this difference. So, the top speed is set to a value of 200 out of 255. Initially, the multipliers are set to 1. You need to adjust your multipliers to fit your robot.

Behavior

The robot is a simple random roamer. It drives in a straight line until it detects an obstacle. It then adjusts its course to avoid striking the obstacle. This is not intended to be a particularly sophisticated solution, but it illustrates some basics in robot operation.

Here are the rules for the robot's behavior:

- It drives forward.

- If it detects an object to its left, it turns right.

- If it detects an object to its right, it turns left.

- If it detects an object directly in front of it, it stops and turns in the direction with the largest distance available.

- If both directions have an equal distance, or both side sensors are beyond the cutoff value, the robot turns in a random direction for a predetermined time before continuing.

This behavior is somewhat basic, but it should provide a robot that wanders about the house autonomously.

The Code

The code is broken into two parts: for the Arduino and for the Pi. On the Arduino, all we care about is operating the sensors and relaying the readings back to the Pi at a predetermined interval. In this case, every 500 milliseconds, or half a second.

The Raspberry Pi uses the incoming data to execute the behavior. It reads from the serial port and parses the data into variables. These variables are used by the Pi to determine the next course of action. This action is translated into instructions for the motors, which are then sent to the motor controller to execute.

Arduino Code

This program simply operates the three ultrasonic sensors on the front of
the robot. It then returns these values as a string of floats to the Raspberry
Pi via the serial connection. The code is essentially the same as the
Pinguino example in Chapter 5. The difference is that we are using three
sensors instead of the one.

1. Open a new sketch in the Arduino IDE.

2. Save the sketch as robot_sensors.

3. Enter the following code:

```
int trigMid = 2;
int echoMid = 3;
int trigLeft = 4;
int echoLeft = 5;
int trigRight = 6;
int echoRight = 7;
float distMid = 0.0;
float distLeft = 0.0;
float distRight = 0.0;
String serialString;

void setup() {
  // set the pinModes for the sensors
  pinMode(trigMid, OUTPUT);
  pinMode(echoMid, INPUT);
  pinMode(trigLeft, OUTPUT);
  pinMode(echoLeft, INPUT);
  pinMode(trigRight, OUTPUT);
  pinMode(echoRight, INPUT);
```

```
  // set trig pins to low;
  digitalWrite(trigMid,LOW);
  digitalWrite(trigLeft,LOW);
  digitalWrite(trigRight,LOW);

  // starting serial
  Serial.begin(115200);
}

// function to operate the sensors
// returns distance in centimeters
float ping(int trigPin, int echoPin){
  // Private variables, not available
  // outside the function
  int duration = 0;
  float distance = 0.0;

  // operate sensor
  digitalWrite(trigPin, HIGH);
  delayMicroseconds(10);
  digitalWrite(trigPin, LOW);

  // get results and calculate distance
  duration = pulseIn(echoPin, HIGH);
  distance = duration/58.2;

  // return the results
  return distance;
}

void loop() {
  // get the distance for each sensor
  distMid = ping(trigMid, echoMid);
  distLeft = ping(trigLeft, echoLeft);
  distRight = ping(trigRight, echoRight);
```

```
    // write the results to the serial port
    Serial.print(distMid); Serial.print(",");
    Serial.print(distLeft); Serial.print(",");
    Serial.println(distRight);

    // wait 500 milliseconds before looping
    delay(500);
}
```

4. Save the sketch and upload it to the Arduino.

The Arduino should now be pinging away, but since there is nothing listening, we don't really know yet. Next, we'll write the code for the Raspberry Pi.

Raspberry Pi Code

It's now time to write the code that runs on the Raspberry Pi. This is a fairly lengthy program, so I'll break it down as we go. The vast majority of this should look very familiar. There are a few changes here and there to accommodate the logic, but for the most part, we've done this before. Whenever we do something new, I'll take the time to walk you through it.

1. Open IDLE for Python 2.7. Remember, the Adafruit library does not work yet in Python 3.

2. Create a new file.

3. Save it as pi_roamer_01.py.

4. Enter the following code. I step through each portion to make sure that you have a solid idea of what is happening along the way.

5. Import the libraries that you need.

```
import serial
import time
import random

from Adafruit_MotorHAT import Adafruit_MotorHAT as amhat
from Adafruit_MotorHAT import Adafruit_DCMotor as adamo
```

6. Create the motor variables and open the serial port. The Arduino is set up to run at a higher baud rate, so the Pi also needs to run at a higher baud.

```
# create motor objects
motHAT = amhat(addr=0x60)
mot1 = motHAT.getMotor(1)
mot2 = motHAT.getMotor(2)
mot3 = motHAT.getMotor(3)
mot4 = motHAT.getMotor(4)

# open serial port
ser = serial.Serial('/dev/ttyACM0', 115200)
```

7. Create the variables needed. Many of them are floats because we are working with decimals.

```
# create variables
# sensors
distMid = 0.0
distLeft = 0.0
distRight = 0.0

# motor multipliers
m1Mult = 1.0
m2Mult = 1.0
m3Mult = 1.0
m4Mult = 1.0
```

```
# distance threshold
distThresh = 12.0
distCutOff = 30.0
```

8. Set up the variables needed to manage the motors.

   You'll note that I have created a number of default values, and then assigned those values to other variables. The leftSpeed, rightSpeed, and driveTime variables should be the only ones that we actually change in code. The rest are to provide consistency throughout the program. If you want to change the default speed, you can simply change speedDef, and the change is applied everywhere.

```
# speeds
speedDef = 200
leftSpeed = speedDef
rightSpeed = speedDef
turnTime = 1.0
defTime = 0.1
driveTime = defTime
```

9. Create the drive function. It is called from two places within the main body of the program. Because there is a lot of work involved, it is better to breakout the code into a separate function block.

```
def driveMotors(leftChnl = speedDef, rightChnl =
speedDef, duration = defTime):
    # determine the speed of each motor by multiplying
    # the channel by the motors multiplier
    m1Speed = leftChnl * m1Mult
    m2Speed = leftChnl * m2Mult
```

```
m3Speed = rightChnl * m3Mult
m4Speed = rightChnl * m4Mult

# set each motor speed. Since the speed can be a
# negative number, we take the absolute value
mot1.setSpeed(abs(int(m1Speed)))
mot2.setSpeed(abs(int(m2Speed)))
mot3.setSpeed(abs(int(m3Speed)))
mot4.setSpeed(abs(int(m4Speed)))

# run the motors. if the channel is negative, run
# reverse. else run forward
if(leftChnl < 0):
    mot1.run(amhat.BACKWARD)
    mot2.run(amhat.BACKWARD)
else:
    mot1.run(amhat.FORWARD)
    mot2.run(amhat.FORWARD)

if (rightChnl > 0):
    mot3.run(amhat.BACKWARD)
    mot4.run(amhat.BACKWARD)
else:
    mot3.run(amhat.FORWARD)
    mot4.run(amhat.FORWARD)

# wait for duration
time.sleep(duration)
```

10. Begin the main block of the program by wrapping
    the code in a try block. This allows us to cleanly
    exit the program. Without it and the corresponding
    except block, the motors would continue to execute
    the last command they received.

```
try:
    while 1:
```

11. Continue the main block by reading the serial port
    and parsing the received string

```
# read the serial port
val = ser.readline().decode('utf=8')
print val

# parse the serial string
parsed = val.split(',')
parsed = [x.rstrip() for x in parsed]

# only assign new values if there are
# three or more available
if(len(parsed)>2):
    distMid = float(parsed[0] + str(0))
    distLeft = float(parsed[1] + str(0))
    distRight = float(parsed[2] + str(0))
```

12. Enter the logic code. This is the code that executes
    the behavior outlined earlier.

    Note that the midsensor block (the one that
    executes a stop and turn) is written outside the left
    and right obstacle avoidance code.

    This is done because we want this logic to be
    evaluated regardless of the outcome of the left and
    right code. By including it after the other code, the
    midcode overwrites any of the values that the left/
    right code created.

```python
# apply cutoff distance
if(distMid > distCutOff):
    distMid = distCutOff
if(distLeft > distCutOff):
    distLeft = distCutOff
if(distRight > distCutOff):
    distRight = distCutOff

# reset driveTime
driveTime = defTime

# if obstacle to left, steer right by increasing
# leftSpeed and running rightSpeed negative defSpeed
# if obstacle to right, steer to left by increasing
# rightSpeed and running leftSpeed negative
if(distLeft <= distThresh):
    leftSpeed = speedDef
    rightSpeed = -speedDef
elif (distRight <= distThresh):
    leftSpeed = -speedDef
    rightSpeed = speedDef
else:
    leftSpeed = speedDef
    rightSpeed = speedDef

# if obstacle dead ahead, stop then turn toward most
# open direction. if both directions open, turn random
if(distMid <= distThresh):
    # stop
    leftSpeed = 0
    rightSpeed = 0
    driveMotors(leftSpeed, rightSpeed, 1)
    time.sleep(1)
```

```
            leftSpeed = -150
            rightSpeed = -150
            driveMotors(leftSpeed, rightSpeed, 1)
            # determine preferred direction. if distLeft >
            # distRight, turn left. if distRight > distLeft,
            # turn right. if equal, turn random
            dirPref = distRight - distLeft
            if(dirPref == 0):
                dirPref = random.random()
            if(dirPref < 0):
                leftSpeed = -speedDef
                rightSpeed = speedDef
            elif(dirPref > 0):
                leftSpeed = speedDef
                rightSpeed = -speedDef
            driveTime = turnTime
```

13. Call the driveMotors function that we created earlier.

```
# drive the motors
driveMotors(leftSpeed, rightSpeed, driveTime)
```

14. Flush any bytes still in the serial buffer.

```
ser.flushInput()
```

15. Enter the except block. It allows us to shut off the motors when we click Ctrl-C before we exit the program.

```
except KeyboardInterrupt:
    mot1.run(amhat.RELEASE)
    mot2.run(amhat.RELEASE)
    mot3.run(amhat.RELEASE)
    mot4.run(amhat.RELEASE)
```

16.   Save the file.

17.   Press F5 to run the program.

When you're done watching your little robot roam around the room, press Ctrl-C to end the program.

Congratulations. You've just built and programmed your first Raspberry Pi–powered robot.

We did a lot in this program—although there was really nothing that you hadn't seen before. In the first part of the program, we imported the libraries that we need and created the motor objects. In the next section, we defined all of our variables. An important part of the program is the function that we created after the variables. In this function we drive the motors. The motor speeds and drive time are passed as parameters of the function which are used to set the speed of each motor. We use the sign of the speed to determine the motor direction. After that, we started our main block by wrapping it in a `try` block. We then entered the `while` loop, which allows the program to repeat indefinitely.

Within the `while` loop, we start by reading the serial string, and then we parse it to extract the three float values. The algorithm for converting the string to a float is a little different from what we used to convert to an integer. More specifically, we did not have to divide the result by 10. Adding a 0 to the end of a decimal does not change the value, so we can use it as it is converted.

The distance measurements determine the robot's next action. The `if/elsif/else` block evaluates the sensor values. If either the left or the right sensor detects an obstacle within the predefined threshold, the robot turns in the opposite direction. If there is no obstacle detected, the robot continues forward. A separate `if` block determines if an obstacle is directly in front of the robot. If there is an obstacle, the robot stops and then turns. It uses the left and right sensor values to determine which way to go. If a direction cannot be determined, the robot turns in a random direction.

All of this takes time, during which the Arduino is happily sending serial strings and filling the Pi's buffer. These strings must be purged before continuing. We use the `flushInput()` method of the serial object to do this. This way, we are working with only the most recent information.

Finally, we use the `except` block to capture the keyboard interrupt command. When it is received, the motors are released, stopping them. Then the program exits.

Summary

This chapter was about bringing together everything we learned so far into a working robot. We assembled the robot chassis kit and mounted all the electronics. Once everything was mounted to the robot, we wrote a program to run the robot. It was a fairly simple roaming program. When you run it, your new robot should wander about the room with varied success, depending on how crowded with furniture the room is.

In the next chapters, we work on improving the robot—adding more sensors, improving the logic, and adding some higher-level functionality. Specifically, we'll be adding a camera and learning how to use OpenCV to track colors and chase a ball.

CHAPTER 8

Working with Infrared Sensors

By this point in the series, you should have a working robot. In previous chapters, I covered everything you need to know to install and program your robot. You've worked with motors, sensors, and communication between the Raspberry Pi and the Arduino. In Chapter 3 and Chapter 5, you learned to work with ultrasonic rangefinders using both Python and Arduino. The remainder of the book introduces new sensors, processing algorithms, and computer vision.

In this chapter, we work with infrared (IR) sensors. We look at different types of sensors. At the end of the chapter, we use a series of IR sensors to detect the edge of a surface and a line.

Infrared Sensors

An infrared (IR) sensor is any sensor that uses a light detector, tuned for the IR spectrum, to detect an IR signal. Generally, the IR sensor is paired with IR-emitting LED to provide the IR signal. The emissions from the LED are measured for intensity or presence.

© Jeff Cicolani 2018
J. Cicolani, *Beginning Robotics with Raspberry Pi and Arduino*,
https://doi.org/10.1007/978-1-4842-3462-4_8

Types of IR Sensors

Infrared is fairly easy to use. As such, we have found many different ways of using it. There is a broad range of IR sensors available. Many are used in applications that you may not expect. Automatic doors, like those seen at retail stores, use a type of sensor called PIR, or *passive infrared*, to detect motion. This type of sensor is used for automatic lights and security systems. Inkjet printers use an IR sensor and an IR-emitting LED to measure the precise movement of the print head. Your entertainment system's remote control likely uses an infrared LED to transmit encoded pulses to an IR receiver. IR-sensitive cameras are used for quality assurance in manufacturing. The list goes on. Let's take a look at some of the different types of IR sensors.

Reflectance Sensors

Reflectance sensors include any sensor designed to detect a signal reflected off a target. Ultrasonic rangefinders are reflectance sensors because they detect the wavelength of sound that is bounced off objects in front of them. IR reflectance sensors work in a similar fashion in that they read the intensity of IR radiation reflected off an object (see Figure 8-1).

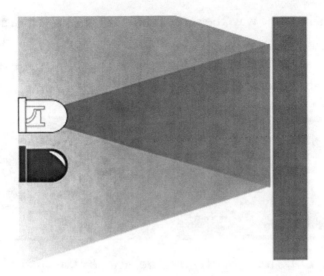

Figure 8-1. *Reflectance sensors measure the IR light returned from an IR diode*

A variant of this type of sensor is designed to detect the presence of an IR signal. The sensor uses a threshold of IR intensity to determine whether or not an object is nearby. The sensor returns a low signal until the threshold is exceeded, at which point it returns a high signal. These sensors are generally paired with an emitting LED, either in a reflected or direct configuration.

Line and Edge Detection

Infrared detectors are frequently used for build devices that detect edges on a line or a ledge. These sensors are used for line detection when the contrast between the surface and the line are high; for instance, a black line on a white table. When the sensor is over the white surface, most of the IR signal is returned to the sensor. When the sensor is over the dark line, less of the IR signal is returned. These sensors usually return an analog signal representing the amount of light returned.

In much the same way, the sensor can detect the edge of a surface. When the sensor is over the surface, the sensor receives more IR signal. When the sensor is over an edge, the signal is greatly reduced, resulting in a low value (see Figure 8-2).

Figure 8-2. *Lines and edges can be detected by the difference in reflected light*

Some sensors have an adjustable threshold, allowing them to provide a digital signal. When the reflectance is above the threshold, the sensor is in a high state. When the reflectance is below the threshold, the sensor is low.

The challenge with this type of sensor is that it can be difficult to dial in the exact threshold to get consistent results. Then, even if you do get them dialed in for one environment, as soon as the conditions change, or you try to demo it at an event, they have to be recalibrated. (Not that this has happened to me repeatedly.) Because of this, I prefer to use analog sensors, which allow me to include an autocalibration procedure so that the program can set its own thresholds.

Rangefinders

Much like proximity sensors, *rangefinders* measure the distance to an object. Rangefinders use a stronger LED with a narrower beam, which is used to determine the approximate range to an object. Unlike ultrasonic rangefinders, IR rangefinders are designed to detect a specific range. It is important to match the sensor to the application.

Interrupt Sensors

Interrupt sensors are used to detect the presence of an IR signal. They are usually paired with an emitting diode and configured to allow an object to pass between the emitter and the detector. When the object is present and blocking the emitter, the receiver returns a low signal. When the object is not present, and the receiver is allowed to detect the emitter, the signal is high.

These sensors are frequently used in devices known as *encoders*. An encoder generally consists of a disc or tape with translucent and transparent sections. As the disc or tape moves past the sensor, the signal continuously goes from high to low. A microcontroller, or other electronics, can then use this alternating signal to count the pulses. Because the number of transparent sections is known, the movement can be calculated with high confidence. In their simplest form, these sensors can only provide a pulse for the microcontroller to count. Some encoders use a number of sensors to provide precise information about movement, including direction.

PIR Motion Detectors

Another, very common, sensor is known as a *PIR motion detector* (see Figure 8-3). These sensors have a faceted lens that reflects and refracts the IR radiation emitted or reflected by an object onto IR sensors within it. When a change is detected by these sensors, a high signal is produced.

Figure 8-3. *Common PIR sensor*

These sensors control the automatic doors at your local grocery store, and operate the automatic lights in your home or office.

Working with IR Sensors

As I discussed earlier, there are a few ways to work with IR sensors, depending on the type you're using. For our project, we'll use five IR line sensors like those shown in Figure 8-4. The sensors I prefer working with are the analog type. The particular sensor that we use can actually do both analog and digital readings. It has a small potentiometer that sets the threshold; however, as I discussed earlier in this chapter, these are notoriously difficult to dial in. I much prefer using the analog readings, directly, and calculating the thresholds in software.

Figure 8-4. *IR sensors for line following*

Connecting an IR Sensor

The sensor that I used for my robot is a 4-pin variant of the common 3-pin IR sensor. The 3-pin sensors are digital and apply a threshold to the analog signal of the sensor to return a high or a low signal. The 4-pin version uses the same threshold setting to return a digital signal, but it also has an additional pin that provides the analog reading. Let's walk through using both signals.

The sensors I use are a little different than most. They were specifically designed for use in line-following applications. As such, the return values are inverted. This means that rather than providing high numbers when the reflectance is high, it returns low numbers. In the same vein, the digital signal is also inverted. A high value indicates the presence of a line and a low value indicates white space. When you run the next exercise, don't be surprised if your results are different. We are looking for fairly consistent behavior.

We will connect the 4-pin sensor to the Arduino and use the serial monitor to see the output of the sensor. We could use a digital pin for the high/low signal and an analog pin for the analog sensor, but to make the wiring easier, we use two of the analog pins. The analog pin connected to the digital output is used in digital mode, so it acts exactly like the other pins.

Since the Arduino is now mounted on the robot, let's use the sensor shield for the connections. Also, I'm not going to disconnect the ultrasonic rangefinders. The sketch for the IR sensors doesn't use those pins, so there is no reason to disconnect them.

For this exercise, you also need a test surface. A white sheet of paper with a large black area or a thick black line works best. Since most line-following contests use 3/4-inch black electrical tape for the line, putting a strip of this tape on a sheet of paper, white poster board, or foam core board is ideal.

1. Using a female-to-female jumper, connect the ground pin of the sensor to the ground pin of the A0 3-pin header.

2. Connect the VCC pin of the sensor to the voltage pin of the 3-pin header A0. This is the middle pin.

3. Connect the analog pin to the signal pin for A0. (On my sensor, the analog pin is labeled A0.)

4. Connect the sensor's digital pin to A1's signal pin. (On my sensor, it is labeled D0.)

5. Create a new sketch in the Arduino IDE.

6. Save the sketch as IR_test.

7. Enter the following code:

```
int analogPin = A0;
int digitalPin = A1;

float analogVal = 0.0;
int digitalVal = 0;

void setup() {
  pinMode(analogPin, INPUT);
  pinMode(digitalPin, INPUT);

  Serial.begin(9600);
}

void loop() {
  analogVal = analogRead(analogPin);
  digitalVal = digitalRead(digitalPin);

  Serial.print("analogVal: "); Serial.print(analogVal);
  Serial.print(" - digitalVal: "); Serial.
  println(digitalVal);

  delay(500);
}
```

8. Move the sensor over the white area of your surface. The sensor needs to be very close to the surface without touching it.

9. Note the values being returned. (I got analog values in the 30 to 45 range. My digital value was 0.)

10. Move the sensor over the line or another black area on the surface.

11. Note the values. (I got analog values in the 700 to 900 range. The digital value was 1.)

You should have received very different values between the light and dark areas of your surface. You can see how this is easily translated into very useful functionality.

Mounting the IR Sensors

Next, we're going to mount the sensors onto the robot to do something useful. Again, since your build may vary greatly from mine, I will walk through what I did to connect the sensors. If you've been faithfully following along, then you should replicate what I've done. If not, then this is where robotics starts to get creative. You need to determine how to mount the sensors onto your robot. Take a look at my solution to get an idea of what you're looking for.

To mount the sensors, I turned (once again) to the parts in the Erector Set. These parts are incredibly convenient and easy to use. In this case, I used one of the bars and the same angle bracket used to mount the ultrasonic rangefinders. In fact, by using the angle bracket, I extended that assembly to bring the IR sensors closer to the ground.

In attempting to then mount the IR sensors, I encountered an issue. The hole for mounting the sensor is between two surface mount resistors. This means a metal standoff would likely cause a short. The nylon standoffs in my inventory are too large to lay flat in that space. I can use spacers and a long screw, but the spacers are too narrow and won't sit straight against the holes in the mounting bar. Adding washers brings the sensors too close to the ground.

The solution was to mount the IR sensors on top of the bar. The challenge was that the solder joints of the pins would definitely short against the metal bar. But, that was easily resolved by putting a piece of electrical tape on the back of the sensor and poking a hole for the mount screw (see Figure 8-5).

Figure 8-5. *Mounting the IR sensors on a bar. Electrical tape protects the leads from shorting.*

Once the sensors were mounted, I needed to run the leads from the sensors to the Arduino board. I only used the analog pin of the sensors, so I needed to use one logic pin on the Arduino for each. If I used both the analog and digital pins, I would need corresponding analog and digital pins on the Arduino. So, I used pins A0 through A4. To make sure that the leads reached properly, without putting undo strain on the connections, I used shorter male-to-female jumpers to extend them. A little tape around the connections and the sensors were ready to go (see Figure 8-6).

Figure 8-6. *The completed robot with IR sensors mounted and wired*

The Code

This project, like the last, uses the Arduino as the GPIO device. The majority of the logic is performed by the Raspberry Pi. We will read the IR sensors in 10-millisecond intervals, 100 times per second. These values are passed to the Raspberry Pi to work with. As you saw in an earlier exercise, reading the sensors is very easy, so the Arduino code is pretty light.

The Pi side is significantly more complex. First, we have to calibrate the sensors. Then, once calibrated, we have to write an algorithm that uses the readings from the sensors to keep the robot on a line. This may be more complicated than you expect. Later in this chapter we look at a good solution, but for now, we'll use a more direct approach.

Arduino Code

The Arduino code is very simple for this application. We will read each of the sensors and send the results to the Pi via the serial connection, 100 times per second. However, since we need the sensor readings more frequently during calibration, we need to know when the calibration is being run because we want the updates to occur 100 times per second to make sure that we get good results.

1. Start a new sketch in the Arduino IDE.

2. Save the sketch as line_follow1.

3. Enter the following code:

```
int ir1Pin = A0;
int ir2Pin = A1;
int ir3Pin = A2;
int ir4Pin = A3;
int ir5Pin = A4;

int ir1Val = 0;
int ir2Val = 0;
int ir3Val = 0;
int ir4Val = 0;
int ir5Val = 0;

void setup() {
  pinMode(ir1Pin, INPUT);
  pinMode(ir2Pin, INPUT);
  pinMode(ir3Pin, INPUT);
  pinMode(ir4Pin, INPUT);
  pinMode(ir5Pin, INPUT);

  Serial.begin(9600);
}
```

```
void loop() {
  ir1Val = analogRead(ir1Pin);
  ir2Val = analogRead(ir2Pin);
  ir3Val = analogRead(ir3Pin);
  ir4Val = analogRead(ir4Pin);
  ir5Val = analogRead(ir5Pin);

  Serial.print(ir1Val); Serial.print(",");
  Serial.print(ir2Val); Serial.print(",");
  Serial.print(ir3Val); Serial.print(",");
  Serial.print(ir4Val); Serial.print(",");
  Serial.println(ir5Val);

  delay(100);
}
```

4.   Save and upload the sketch.

This sketch is very straightforward. All we are doing is reading each of the five sensors and printing the results to the serial port.

Python Code

Most of the processing is done on the Pi. The first thing we need to do is calibrate the sensors to get the high and low values. To do that, we need to sweep the sensors back and forth over the line while we read the values from each sensor. We are looking for the highest and lowest values. Once we've done a few passes over the line, we should have good values to work with.

With the sensors calibrated, it's time to start moving. Drive the robot forward. As long as the line is detected by the middle sensor, just keep driving forward. If one of the sensors to the left or right reads the line, make a slight correction the opposite direction to realign. If one of the outside sensors reads the line, make a more dramatic correction. This keeps the robot following along the line and handling easy turns.

To run this code properly, make a line for it to follow. There are several ways to do this. If you happen to have a white tile floor, then you can put electrical tape directly on it. Electrical tape lifts from the tile without damaging it. Otherwise, you can use sheets of paper, poster board, or foam core board like those used for science fair displays. Again, use electrical tape to mark the line. Be sure to add some curves.

As with the roamer code, we'll walk through this in parts. The code that we are writing is getting lengthier.

1. Open a new file in the IDLE IDE.

2. Save the file as line_follow1.py.

3. Import the necessary libraries:

```
import serial
import time

from Adafruit_MotorHAT import Adafruit_MotorHAT as amhat
from Adafruit_MotorHAT import Adafruit_DCMotor as adamo
```

4. Create the motor objects. To make the code more Pythonic, let's put the motor objects in a list.

```
# create motor objects
motHAT = amhat(addr=0x60)
mot1 = motHAT.getMotor(1)
mot2 = motHAT.getMotor(2)
mot3 = motHAT.getMotor(3)
mot4 = motHAT.getMotor(4)

motors = [mot1, mot2, mot3, mot4]
```

5. Define the variables needed to control the motors. Again, let's create lists.

```
# motor multipliers
motorMultiplier = [1.0, 1.0, 1.0, 1.0, 1.0]

# motor speeds
motorSpeed = [0,0,0,0]
```

6. Open the serial port.

```
# open serial port
ser = serial.Serial('/dev/ttyACM0', 9600)
```

7. Define the necessary variables. As with the motors, define some of the variables as lists. (This pays off later in the code. I promise.)

```
# create variables
# sensors
irSensors = [0,0,0,0,0]
irMins = [0,0,0,0,0]
irMaxs = [0,0,0,0,0]
irThesh = 50

# speeds
speedDef = 200
leftSpeed = speedDef
rightSpeed = speedDef
corMinor = 50
corMajor = 100
turnTime = 0.5
defTime = 0.01
driveTime = defTime
sweepTime = 1000 #duration of a sweep in milliseconds
```

8. Define the function to drive the motors. Though similar, this code is different from the roamer function.

```
def driveMotors(leftChnl = speedDef, rightChnl = speedDef,
                duration = defTime):
    # determine the speed of each motor by multiplying
    # the channel by the motors multiplier
    motorSpeed[0] = leftChnl * motorMultiplier[0]
    motorSpeed[1] = leftChnl * motorMultiplier[1]
    motorSpeed[2] = rightChnl * motorMultiplier[2]
    motorSpeed[3] = rightChnl * motorMultiplier[3]
```

9. Iterate the motor list to set the speed. Also, iterate the motorSpeed list.

```
    # set each motor speed. Since the speed can be a
    # negative number, we take the absolute value
    for x in range(4):
        motors[x].setSpeed(abs(int(motorSpeed[x])))
```

10. Run the motors.

```
    # run the motors. if the channel is negative, run
    # reverse. else run forward
    if(leftChnl < 0):
        motors[0].run(amhat.BACKWARD)
        motors[1].run(amhat.BACKWARD)
    else:
        motors[0].run(amhat.FORWARD)
        motors[1].run(amhat.FORWARD)

    if (rightChnl > 0):
        motors[2].run(amhat.BACKWARD)
        motors[3].run(amhat.BACKWARD)
```

```
else:
    motors[2].run(amhat.FORWARD)
    motors[3].run(amhat.FORWARD)

# wait for duration
time.sleep(duration)
```

11. Define the function to read the IR sensor values from the serial stream and parse them.

```
def getIR():
    # read the serial port
    val = ser.readline().decode('utf-8')

    # parse the serial string
    parsed = val.split(',')
    parsed = [x.rstrip() for x in parsed]
```

12. Iterate the irSensors list to assign the parsed values, and then flush any remaining bytes from the serial stream.

```
if(len(parsed)==5):
    for x in range(5):
        irSensors[x] = int(parsed[x]+str(0))/10

# flush the serial buffer of any extra bytes
ser.flushInput()
```

13. Define the function to calibrate the sensors. The calibration goes through four complete cycles to read the minimum and maximum values from the sensor.

```
def calibrate():
    # set up cycle count loop
    direction = 1
    cycle = 0

    # get initial values for each sensor
    # and set initial min/max values
    getIR()

    for x in range(5):
        irMins[x] = irSensors[x]
        irMaxs[x] = irSensors[x]
```

14. Loop through the cycle five times to assure that you
    get four full cycle readings.

```
while cycle < 5:

    #set up sweep loop
    millisOld = int(round(time.time()*1000))
    millisNew = millisOld
```

15. For the duration of sweepTime, drive the motors
    and read the IR sensors.

```
while((millisNew-millisOld)<sweepTime):
    leftSpeed = speedDef * direction
    rightSpeed = speedDef * -direction

    # drive the motors
    driveMotors(leftSpeed, rightSpeed, driveTime)

    # read sensors
    getIR()
```

16. Update irMins and irMaxs if the sensor values are below or above the current irMins or irMaxs values.

```
# set min and max values for each sensor
for x in range(5):
    if(irSensors[x] < irMins[x]):
        irMins[x] = irSensors[x]
    elif(irSensors[x] > irMaxs[x]):
        irMaxs[x] = irSensors[x]

millisNew = int(round(time.time()*1000))
```

17. After one cycle, change motor directions and the increment the cycle value.

```
# reverse direction
direction = -direction

# increment cycles
cycle += 1
```

18. When the cycles have completed, drive the robot forward.

```
# drive forward
driveMotors(speedDef, speedDef, driveTime)
```

19. Define the followLine function.

```
def followLine():
    leftSpeed = speedDef
    rightSpeed = speedDef

    getIR()
```

20. Define the behavior based on the senor readings. If the line is detected by the far right or far left sensors, do a major correction in the other direction. If the inner right or inner left sensors detect the line, do a minor correction in the other direction; else, drive straight.

```
# find line and correct if necessary
if(irMaxs[0]-irThresh <= irSensors[0]
<= irMaxs[0]+irThresh):
    leftSpeed = speedDef-corMajor
elif(irMaxs[1]-irThresh <= irSensors[1]
<= irMaxs[1]+irThresh):
    leftSpeed = speedDef-corMinor
elif(irMaxs[3]-irThresh <= irSensors[3]
<= irMaxs[3]+irThresh):
    rightSpeed = speedDef-corMinor
elif(irMaxs[4]-irThresh <= irSensors[4]
<= irMaxs[4]+irThresh):
    rightSpeed = speedDef-corMajor
else:
    leftSpeed = speedDef
    rightSpeed = speedDef

# drive the motors
driveMotors(leftSpeed, rightSpeed, driveTime)
```

21. Enter the code to run the program.

```
# execute program
try:
    calibrate()
```

```
while 1:
    followLine()
    time.sleep(0.01)

except KeyboardInterrupt:
    mot1.run(amhat.RELEASE)
    mot2.run(amhat.RELEASE)
    mot3.run(amhat.RELEASE)
    mot4.run(amhat.RELEASE)
```

22. Save the code.

23. Place the robot on the line. The robot should be
     aligned so that the line runs between the left and
     right wheels, and the center sensor is directly over it.

24. Run the program.

Your robot should now follow along the line, making corrections if it
starts to wander off the line. You probably need to play with the corMinor
and corMajor variables to fine-tune the behavior.

What we executed here is known as *proportional control*. This is the
simplest form of control algorithm. The basic logic behind it is that if your
robot is a little off course, apply a little correction. If the robot is a lot off
course, apply a lot more correction. The amount of correction applied to
the robot is determined by how big the error is.

With proportional control alone, the robot tries really hard to follow
the line. It may even succeed; however, you will note how it zigzags along
the line. This behavior may be reduced over time and become smooth;
however, when you introduce a curve, the erratic behavior starts all over
again. More likely, your robot overcorrected and wandered off in a random
direction, leaving the line far behind.

There is a better way to control the robot. In fact, there are several
better ways, all from a field of study called *control loops*. Control loops
are algorithms to improve the response of a machine or program. Most of

them use the difference between the current state and a desired state to control the machine. This difference is called the *error*.

Let's look at once such control system next.

Understanding PID Control

To better control the robot, you are going to learn about PID control, and I'll try to discuss it without getting math heavy. The PID controller is one of the most widely used control loops because of its versatility and simplicity. We've actually already used part of a PID controller: proportional control. The remaining parts help smooth the reaction and provide a better response.

Control Loops

The PID controller is a member of a group of algorithms called *control loops*. The purpose of a control loop is to use input from a measured process to make changes to a control, or controls, to compensate for differences between the current state and a desired state. There are many different types of control loops. In fact, control loops are a whole area of study called *control theory*. For our purposes, we really only care about one: proportional, integral, and derivative—or PID.

Proportional, Integral, and Derivative Control

According to Wikipedia, a "PID controller continuously calculates an error value (e(t)) as the difference between a desired setpoint and a measured process variable and applies a correction based on proportional, integral, and derivative terms. PID is an initialism for Proportional-Integral-Derivative, referring to the three terms operating on the error signal to produce a control signal."

The purpose of the controller is to apply incremental adjustments to some output to achieve the desired result. In our application, we use the feedback from IR sensors to apply changes to our motors. The desired behavior is a robot that keeps centered on a line as it moves forward. This process can be used with any sensors and outputs, however; for instance, PID is used in multirotor platforms to remain level and maintain stability.

As the name implies, the PID algorithm actually consists of three parts: proportional, integral, and derivative. Each part is a type of control; however, if used independently, the resulting behavior would be erratic and difficult to predict.

Proportional Control

In proportional control, the amount of change is set based entirely on the size of the error. The larger the error, the more change is applied. A purely proportional control would reach a zero-error state, but has difficulty dealing with drastic changes, which results in heavy oscillation.

Integral Control

Integral control considers not only the error, but also the time that it has persisted. The amount of change applied to compensate for the error increases over time. A purely integral control could bring the device to a zero-error state, but it reacts slowly and tends to overcompensate and oscillate.

Derivative Control

Derivative control does not consider the error, and therefore it can never bring the device to a zero-error state. It does try to reduce the change in error to zero, however. If too much compensation is applied, the algorithm overshoots, and then applies another correction. The process continues in this manner, producing a pattern of constantly increasing or decreasing corrections. Although a state of decreasing oscillation is considered "stable," the algorithm never reaches a truly zero-error state.

Bringing Them Together

The PID controller is simply the sum of the three methods. By bringing them together, the algorithm aims to produce a smooth correcting process that brings the error to zero. Time for a little bit of math.

Let's start by defining some variables.

$e(t)$ is the error in time, where (t) is time, or the present.

K_p is a parameter representing the proportional gain. When we start coding, this is the proportional variable.

K_i is the integral gain parameter. It is also a variable.

K_d is the derivative gain parameter. And you guessed it, yet another variable.

τ represents integrated values over time. I'll get to that.

The proportional term is basically the current error multiplied by the K_p value.

$$P_{out} = K_p e(t)$$

The integral portion is a bit more complicated because it takes into account all the errors that have happened. It is the sum of the errors over time and the accumulated correction.

$$I_{out} = K_i \int_0^t e(\tau)\, d\tau$$

The derivative term is the difference between the original error and the current errors over time, and then multiplied by the derivative parameter.

$$D_{out} = K_d \frac{de(t)}{dt}$$

To bring it all together, our PID equation looks like this:

$$u(t)=\left(K_{p}e(t)\right)+\left(K_{i}\int_{0}^{t}e(\tau)d\tau\right)+\left(K_{d}\frac{de(t)}{dt}\right)$$

That's it for the math. Fortunately, we don't have to solve it ourselves. Python makes it very easy. However, it is important to understand what is happening inside the equation. There are three parameters to adjust to fine-tune the PID controller. By understanding how these parameters are used, you will be able to determine which ones need adjusting and when.

Implementing the PID Controller

To implement the controller, we need to know a few things. What is our desired outcome? What are our inputs? What are our outputs?

The goal is to improve the performance of our line-following robot. So, our desired outcome is that the line remains in the center of the robot while it drives forward.

Our inputs are the IR sensors. When an outer sensor is over a dark area (the line), the error is twice that of the inner sensors. In this way, we'll know whether the robot is a little off-center or a lot off-center. Also, the two left sensors will have a negative value, and the right sensors will have a positive value, so we will know which direction is off.

Finally, our outputs are the motors. More accurately, our output is the difference in speed between the left and right motor channels.

The Code

The code for this exercise is a modification of the earlier code. In fact, the Arduino code does not need to change at all. It's the logic we are implementing on the Raspberry Pi that is updated.

Raspberry Pi Code

We will modify the `line_follower1` code to use PID rather than the proportional algorithm. To do that, we need to update the `getIR` function to update a new variable called `sensorErr`. We will then replace the code inside the `followLine` function with our PID code.

1. Open the file `line_follower1` in the IDLE IDE.

2. From the file menu, select **Save as**, and save the file as `line_follower2.py`.

3. In the variables section, under `#sensors`, add the following code:

```
# PID
sensorErr = 0
lastTime = int(round(time.time()*1000))
lastError = 0
target = 0
kp = 0.5
ki = 0.5
kd = 1
```

4. Create the PID function.

```
def PID(err):
    # check if variables are defined before use
    # the first time the PID is called these variables will
    # not have been defined
    try: lastTime
    except NameError: lastTime = int(round(time.
    time()*1000)-1)

    try: sumError
    except NameError: sumError = 0
```

```python
try: lastError
except NameError: lastError = 0

# get the current time
now = int(round(time.time()*1000))
duration = now-lastTime

# calculate the error
error = target - err
sumError += (error * duration)
dError = (error - lastError)/duration

# calculate PID
output = kp * error + ki * sumError + kd * dError

# update variables
lastError = error
lastTime = now

# return the output value
return output
```

5. Replace the followLine function with this:

```python
def followLine():
    leftSpeed = speedDef
    rightSpeed = speedDef

    getIR()

    prString = ''
    for x in range(5):
        prString += ('IR' + str(x) + ': ' +
        str(irSensors[x]) + ' ')
    print prString
```

```
# find line and correct if necessary
if(irMaxs[0]-irThresh <= irSensors[0]
<= irMaxs[0]+irThresh):
    sensorErr = 2
elif(irMaxs[1]-irThresh <= irSensors[1]
<= irMaxs[1]+irThresh):
    sensorErr = 1
elif(irMaxs[3]-irThresh <= irSensors[3]
<= irMaxs[3]+irThresh):
    sensorErr = -1
elif(irMaxs[4]-irThresh <= irSensors[4]
<= irMaxs[4]+irThresh):
    sensorErr = -1
else:
    sensorErr = 0

# get PID results
ratio = PID(sensorErr)

# apply ratio
leftSpeed = speedDef * ratio
rightSpeed = speedDef * -ratio

# drive the motors
driveMotors(leftSpeed, rightSpeed, driveTime)
```

6. Save the file.

7. Place the robot on the line.

8. Run the code.

Once again, your robot should be trying to follow the line. If it is having problems doing so, start working with the K_p, K_i, and K_d variables. These variables need to be fine-tuned for the best results. Every robot is different.

Summary

In this chapter, we added some new sensors to the robot. The IR sensors were applied in a line-following application. They can also be used to detect the edge of a surface. This functionality is useful if you want to prevent your robot from driving off a table or down stairs.

Our first implementation of line following used a basic proportional control to steer the robot. This was functional, but barely. A much better way of doing this was the use of a control loop called the PID controller, which uses several factors, including error over time, to make the corrections smoother. You learned that you can adjust the ID settings by using the PID parameters represented in our code, with the K_p, K_i, and K_d variables. With the proper values, the oscillation can be eliminated completely, causing the robot to follow the line smoothly.

CHAPTER 9

An Introduction to OpenCV

We've come a long way since the first chapters introducing the Raspberry Pi. At this point, you have learned about the Pi and the Arduino. You've learned how to program both boards. You've worked with sensors and motors. You've built your robot and programmed it to roam around and to follow a line.

However, to be completely honest, you haven't really needed the power of the Raspberry Pi. In fact, it's been a bit of hindrance. Everything you've done with the robot—roaming and line following, you could do just well with the Arduino and without Pi. It's now time to show the real power of the Pi and to learn why you want to use it in your robot.

In this chapter, we're going to do something you can't do with the Arduino alone. We are going to connect a simple web camera and start working with what is commonly known as *computer vision*.

Computer Vision

Computer vision is a collection of algorithms that allow a computer to analyze an image and extract useful information. It is used in many applications, and it is rapidly becoming a part of everyday life. If you have a smartphone, chances are you have at least one app that uses computer

© Jeff Cicolani 2018
J. Cicolani, *Beginning Robotics with Raspberry Pi and Arduino*,
https://doi.org/10.1007/978-1-4842-3462-4_9

vision. Most new moderate to high-end cameras have facial detection built in. Facebook uses computer vision for facial detection. Computer vision is used by shipping companies to track packages in their warehouses. And, of course, it's used in robotics for navigation, object detection, object avoidance, and many others behaviors.

It all starts with an image. The computer analyzes an image to identify lines, corners, and a broad area of color. This process is called *feature extraction*, and it is the first step in virtually all computer vision algorithms. Once the features are extracted, the computer can use this information for many different tasks.

Facial recognition is accomplished by comparing the features against XML files containing feature data for faces. These XML files are called *cascades*. They are available for many different types of objects, not just faces. This same technique can be used for object recognition. You simply provide the application with feature information for the objects that interest you.

Computer vision also incorporates video. *Motion tracking* is a common application for computer vision. To detect motion, the computer compares individual frames from a stationary camera. If there is no motion, the features will not change between frames. So, if the computer identifies differences between frames, there is most likely motion. Computer vision–based motion tracking is more reliable than IR sensors, such as the PIR sensor discussed in Chapter 8.

An exciting, recent application of computer vision is augmented reality. The extracted features from a video stream can be used to identify a unique pattern on a surface. Because the computer knows the pattern, it can easily calculate the angle of the surface. A 3D model is then superimposed over the pattern. This 3D model could be something physical, like a building, or it could be a planar object with two-dimensional text. Architects use this technique to show clients what a building would look like against a skyline. Museums use it to provide more information about an exhibit or an artist.

All of these are examples of computer vision in modern settings. But the list of applications is too large to discuss in depth here, and it keeps growing.

OpenCV

Just a few years ago, computer vision was not really accessible to the hobbyist. It required a lot of heavy math and even heavier processing. Computer vision projects were generally done using laptops, which limited its application.

OpenCV has been around for a while. In 1999, Intel Research established an open standard for promoting the development of computer vision. In 2012, it was taken over by the nonprofit OpenCV Foundation. You can download the latest version at their website. It's take a little extra effort to get it running on the Raspberry Pi, however. We'll get to that shortly.

OpenCV is written natively in C++; however, it can be used in C, Java, and Python. We are interested in the Python implementation. Because our motor controller libraries are not Python 3–compatible, we need to install OpenCV for Python 2.7.

Installing OpenCV

We will install OpenCV on the Raspberry Pi. You want to make sure that your Raspberry Pi is plugged into a charger rather than the battery pack, and give yourself plenty of time for the installation. We will compile OpenCV from source, which means that we will download the source code from the Internet and build it directly on the Pi. Be warned that although the process is not difficult, it does take a long time and involves entering many Linux commands. I usually begin the process in the evening and let the final build run overnight.

1. Log on to your Raspberry Pi.

2. Open a terminal window on the Pi.

3. Make sure that the Raspberry Pi is updated.

```
sudo apt-get update
sudo apt-get upgrade
sudo rpi-update
sudo reboot
```

4. These commands install the prerequisites for building OpenCV.

```
sudo apt-get install build-essential git cmake pkg-config
sudo apt-get install libjpeg-dev libtiff5-dev
libjasper-dev libpng12-dev
sudo apt-get install libavcodec-dev libavformat-dev
libswscale-dev libv4l-dev
sudo apt-get install libxvidcore-dev libx264-dev
sudo apt-get install libgtk2.0-dev
sudo apt-get install libatlas-base-dev gfortran
```

5. Download the OpenCV source code and the OpenCV contributed files. The contributed files contain a lot of functionality not yet rolled into the main OpenCV distribution.

```
cd ~
git clone https://github.com/Itseez/opencv.git
cd opencv
git checkout 3.1.0
cd ~
git clone https://github.com/Itseez/opencv_contrib.git
cd opencv_contrib
git checkout 3.1.0
```

6. Install the Python development libraries and pip.

```
sudo apt-get install python2.7-dev
wget https://bootstrap.pypa.io/get-pip.py
sudo python get-pip.py
```

7. Make sure that NumPy is installed.

```
pip install numpy
```

8. Prepare the source code for compiling.

```
cd ~/opencv
mkdir build
cd build
cmake -D CMAKE_BUILD_TYPE=RELEASE \
    -D CMAKE_INSTALL_PREFIX=/usr/local \
    -D INSTALL_C_EXAMPLES=OFF \
    -D INSTALL_PYTHON_EXAMPLES=ON \
    -D OPENCV_EXTRA_MODULES_PATH=~/opencv_contrib/modules \
    -D BUILD_EXAMPLES=ON ..
```

9. Now let's compile the source code. This part is going
    to take a while.

    Some people try to leverage all four cores in the
    Raspberry Pi's ARM CPU. However, I've found this
    to be error prone, and it has never worked for me.
    My suggestion is to just bite the bullet: let the Pi
    determine the number of cores to use and let it run.
    If you want to brave it, you can force the Pi to use four
    cores by adding the -j4 switch to the following line

```
make
```

10. If you attempted the –j4 switch and it failed, somewhere around hour four, enter the following lines:

```
make clean
make
```

11. With the source code compiled, you can now install it.

```
sudo make install
sudo ldconfig
```

12. Test the installation by opening a Python command line.

```
python
```

13. Import OpenCV.

```
>>>import cv2
```

You should now have an operating version of OpenCV installed on your Raspberry Pi. If the import command did not work, you need to determine why it did not install. The Internet is your guide for troubleshooting.

Selecting a Camera

Before we can really put OpenCV to work on our robot, we need to install a camera. There are a couple of options with the Raspberry Pi: the Pi Camera or a USB web camera.

The Pi Camera connects directly to a port designed specifically for it. Once connected, you need to go into raspi-config and enable it. The advantage of the Pi Camera is that it is a little bit faster than a USB camera because it is connected directly to the board. It does not go through the USB serial bus. This gives it a slight advantage.

Most of the Pi Cameras come with a short, 6-inch ribbon cable. Due to the placement of the Raspberry Pi on our robot, this is insufficient. It is possible to order longer cables. Adafruit has a couple of options. But, for this project, we will use a simple web camera.

USB cameras are readily available at any electronics retailer. There are many options online, as well. For this basic application, we won't need anything particularly robust. Any camera that can provide a decent image will do. Having a high resolution is not a concern, either. Since we are running the camera with the limited resources of the Raspberry Pi, a lower resolution would actually help performance. Remember, OpenCV analyzes each frame pixel by pixel. The more pixels there are in an image, the more processing it has to do.

For my robot, I chose the Live! Cam Sync HD by Creative (see Figure 9-1), a basic HD webcam with a built-in microphone that operates via a standard USB 2 port. We won't need the microphone for this project, but there may be a need in the future. It captures 720p HD video, which may be a little much for our robot, but if there is a performance hit, I always reduce the resolution in software.

Figure 9-1.   *Creative Live! Cam Sync HD*

Installing the Camera

Most webcams are mounted on top of a monitor. They usually have a folding clamp to provide support for the camera when on the monitor. Unfortunately, these clamps are usually molded as part of the camera's body and can't be removed without damaging it. This certainly holds true with the Live! Cam Sync. So, once again, a little creativity comes into play.

The bracket I use to mount the sensors comes off the front of the robot at a 45-degree angle. To make things a little easier on myself, I choose not to drill holes in the camera's mount. Rather, I use my trusty mounting tape and a couple of brackets from the Erector Set. When I mount it, I want to get it up fairly high and pointing slightly downward. The idea is to give it the best view forward, and of any objects directly in front of it. I also want the lens to be as close to the center axis as possible to keep things simpler on the software side. Figure 9-2 shows the robot after the camera is mounted.

Figure 9-2. *Camera mounted on robot*

OpenCV Basics

OpenCV has many capabilities. It boasts more than 500 libraries and thousands of functions. It is a very big subject—too large a subject to cover in one chapter. I'll discuss the basics needed to perform some simple tasks on your robot.

I said *simple* tasks. These tasks are only simple because OpenCV abstracts the monumental amount of math that is happening in the background. When I consider the state of hobby robotics a few short years ago, I find it amazing to be able to easily access even the basics.

The goal is to build a robot that can identify a ball and move toward it by the end of this chapter. The functions I cover will help us achieve that goal. I strongly suggest spending time going through some of the tutorials at the OpenCV website (`https://opencv.org`).

To work with OpenCV in your Python code, you need to import it. And, while you're at it, you likely need to import the NumPy library as well. NumPy adds a lot of mathematical and number handling functionality that makes working with OpenCV much easier. All of your image-related code should start with this:

```
import cv2
import numpy as np
```

In the code discussions in this chapter, I assume this has been done. A function prefixed with `cv2` is an OpenCV function. If it's prefixed with `np`, it is a NumPy function. It's important to make this distinction in the event that you want to expand on what you read in this book. OpenCV and NumPy are two separate libraries, but OpenCV frequently uses NumPy.

Working with Images

In this section, you learn how to open images from file and how to capture live video from the camera. We'll then take a look at how to manipulate and analyze the images to get usable information out of them. Specifically, we'll work on how to identify a ball of a particular color and track its position in the frame.

But first, we have a bit of a chicken-or-egg issue. We need to see the results of our image manipulation in all the exercises. To do that, we need to start with how to display an image. It is something that we'll use extensively, and it's very easy to use. But I want to make sure that I cover it first, before you learn how to capture an image.

Displaying an Image

It's actually very easy to display an image in OpenCV. The `imshow()` function provides this functionality. This function is used with both still and video images, and the implementation does not change between them. The imshow() function opens a new window to display the image. When you call it, you have to provide a name for the window as well as the image or frame that you want to display.

This is an important point about how OpenCV works with video. Because OpenCV treats a video as a series of individual frames, virtually all the functions used to modify or analyze an image apply to a video. This obviously includes imshow().

If we want to display an image that we loaded into the img variable, it would look something like this:

```
cv2.imshow('img', img)
```

In this example, the first parameter is the name of the window. It appears in the title bar of the window. The second parameter is the variable holding our image. The format for displaying a video is exactly the same. I usually use the variable cap for video capture, so the code would look like this:

```
cv2.imshow('cap', cap)
```

As you can see, the code is the same. Again, this is because OpenCV treats video as a series of individual frames. In fact, video capture depends on a loop to continuously capture the next frame. So in essence, displaying a still image from a file and an individual frame from the camera is exactly the same thing.

There is one element remaining for an image to display. To actually display the image, the imshow() function requires that waitKey() also be called. The waitKey() function waits for the specified number of milliseconds for a keyboard key to be pressed. Many people use this to capture a Quit key. I generally pass it zero unless I need the keypress.

```
cv2.waitKey(0)
```

We use imshow() and waitKey() extensively throughout this chapter.

Capturing Images

There are several sources for the images needed to work with OpenCV, all of which are a variation of two factors: file or camera, and still or video. For the most part, we are only concerned with video from a camera since we are using OpenCV for navigation purposes. But there are advantages to all the methods.

Opening a still image file is an excellent way to learn new techniques, especially when you are working with specific aspects of computer vision. For example, if you are learning how to use filters to identify a ball of a certain color, using a still image that consists of three different colored balls (and nothing else) allows you to focus on that specific goal without having to worry about the underlying framework for capturing a live video stream. Oh, and that was a bit of foreshadowing, if you hadn't picked up on that.

The techniques learned from capturing a still image with a camera can be applied to a live environment. It allows you to the hone or fine-tune the code by using an image that contains elements of the real world.

Obviously, capturing live video is what we're after for use in the robot. The live video stream is what we'll use to identify our target object and then navigate to it. As your computer vision experience grows, you will probably add motion detection or other methods to your repertoire. Since the purpose of the camera on the robot is to gather environmental information in real time, live video is required.

Video from a file is also very useful for the learning process. You may want to capture live video from your robot and save it to a file for later analysis. Let's say that you are working on your robot project in whatever spare time you are able to find throughout the day. You can port your laptop with you, but carting a robot around is a different story. So, if you record the video from your robot, you can work on your computer vision algorithms without having the robot with you.

Remember, one of the great things about Python and OpenCV is that they're abstracted and platform independent, for the most part. So, the code you write on your Windows machine ports to your Raspberry Pi.

Going on a business trip and expect some downtime in the hotel? Heading to the family's place for the holidays and need to get away every once in a while? Slipping in a little robot programming during your lunch hour or between classes? Use the recorded video with a local instance of Python and OpenCV, and work on your detection algorithm. When you get home, you can transfer that code to your robot and test it live.

In this section, we use the first three techniques. I show you how to save and open video files, but for the most part, we'll use stills to learn the detection algorithm and the live video to learn tracking.

Opening an Image File

OpenCV makes working with images and files remarkably easy, especially considering what is happening in the background to make these operations possible. Opening an image file is no different. We use the `imread()` function to open image files from local storage. The `imread()` function takes two parameters: file name and color type flag. The file name is obviously required to open the file. The color type flag determines whether to open the image in color or grayscale.

Let's open and display an image. I will use an image of three colored balls that is also used later in the chapter to learn how to detect colors. This exercise can be done on the Pi or on your computer if you've installed Python and OpenCV on it.

1. Open the IDLE IDE and create a new file.

2. Save the file as `open_image.py`.

3. Enter the following code:

```
import cv2

img = cv2.imread('color_balls_small.jpg')
cv2.imshow('image',img)

cv2.waitKey(0)
```

4. Save the file.

5. Open a terminal window.

6. Navigate to the folder in which you saved the file.

7. Enter python open_image.py and press Return.

A window opens to show an image of three colored balls on a white background (see Figure 9-3). Press any key to close it.

Figure 9-3. *Three colored balls*

Due to the way IDLE interacts with the GUI system on Linux-based machines, the image window will not close properly if you were to run the code directly from IDLE. However, by running the code from the terminal, we do not have this issue.

Capturing Video

Capturing video with your camera is a little different from opening a file. There are a few more steps to use video. One change is that we have to use a loop to get multiple frames; otherwise, the OpenCV will only capture a single frame, which is not what we want. An open while loop is generally used. This captures the video until we actively stop it.

To make things easier for testing, I placed the ball directly in front of the camera (see Figure 9-4). Right now, we just want to capture the image.

Figure 9-4. *Ball positioned in front of the robot for testing*

To capture the video from the camera, we will create a `videoCapture()` object and then use the `read()` method in a loop to capture the frames. The `read()` method returns two objects: a return value and an image frame. The return value is simply an integer verifying the success or failure of the read. If the read is successful, the value is 1; otherwise, the read failed and it returns 0. To prevent errors that cause your code to error, you can test to see if the read is successful.

We care about the image frame. If the read is successful, an image is returned. If it was not, then a null object is returned in its place. Since a null object cannot access OpenCV methods, the instant you try to modify or manipulate the image, your code will crash. This is why it's a good idea to test for the success of the read operation.

Viewing the Camera

In this next exercise, we turn on the video camera mounted earlier to view the video.

1. Open the IDLE IDE and create a new file.

2. Save the file as view_camera.py.

3. Enter the following code:

```
import cv2
import numpy as np

cap = cv2.VideoCapture(0)

while(True):
    ret,frame = cap.read()

    cv2.imshow('video', frame)
    if cv2.waitKey(1) & 0xff == ord('q'):
        break
```

```
cap.release()
cv2.destroyAllWindows()
```

4. Save the file.

5. Open a terminal window.

6. Navigate to your working folder where the script is saved.

7. Type **sudo python view_camera.py**.

This opens a window displaying what your camera sees. If you are using a remote desktop session to work on the Pi, you may see this warning message: Xlib: extension RANR missing on display :10. This message means that the system is looking for functionality not included in vncserver. It can be ignored.

If you are concerned about the refresh rate of the video image, keep in mind that we are asking an awful lot of the Raspberry Pi when we run several windows through a remote desktop session. If you connect a monitor and keyboard to access the Pi, it runs much faster. The video capture works faster if you run it with no visualization.

Recording Video

Recording a video is an extension of viewing the camera. To record, you have to declare the video codec that you will use, and then set up the VideoWriter object that writes the incoming video the SD card.

OpenCV uses the FOURCC code to designate the codec. FOURCC is a four-character code for a video codec. You can find more information about FOURCC at www.fourcc.org.

When creating the VideoWriter object, we need to provide some information. First, we have to provide the name of the file to save the video. Next, we provide the codec, followed by the frame rate and the resolution. Once the VideoWriter object is created, we simply have to write each from to the file using the write() method of the VideoWriter object.

Let's record some of our robot's video feed. We will use the XVID codec to write to a file called `test_video.avi`. Rather than starting from scratch, we'll use the video capture code from the previous exercise.

1. Open the view_camera.py file in the IDLE IDE.

2. Select File ➤ Save as and save the file as `record_camera.py`.

3. Update the code. In the following, the new lines are in bold:

```
import cv2
import numpy as np

cap = cv2.VideoCapture(0)
fourcc = cv2.VideoWriter_fourcc(*'XVID')
vidWrite = cv2.VideoWriter('test_video.avi', \
                fourcc, 20, (640,480))

while(True):
    ret,frame = cap.read()

    vidWrite.write(frame)

    cv2.imshow('video', frame)
    if cv2.waitKey(1) & 0xff == ord('q'):
        break

cap.release()
vidWrite.release()
cv2.destroyAllWindows()
```

4. Save the file.

5. Open a terminal window.

6. Navigate to your working folder where the script is saved.

7. Type **sudo python record_camera.py**.

8. Let the video run for a few seconds, and then press Q to end the program and close the window.

You should now have a video file in your working directory. Next, we'll look at reading a video from a file.

There are a couple items to note in the code. When we created the VideoWriter object, we supplied the video resolution as a tuple. This is a very common practice throughout OpenCV. Also, we had to release the VideoWriter object. This closed the file from writing.

Reading Video from a File

Playing a video back from a file is exactly the same as viewing a video from a camera. The only difference is that rather than providing the index to a video device, we provide the name of the file to play. We will use the ret variable to test for the end of the video file; otherwise, we would get an error when there is no more video to play.

In this exercise, we are simply going to play back the video that we recorded in the previous exercise. The code should look remarkably familiar.

1. Open the IDLE IDE and create a new file.

2. Save the file as view_video.py.

3. Enter the following code:

```
import cv2
import numpy as np

cap = cv2.VideoCapture('test_video.avi')
```

```
while(True):
    ret,frame = cap.read()

    if ret:
        cv2.imshow('video', frame)
    if cv2.waitKey(1) & 0xff == ord('q'):
        break

cap.release()
cv2.destroyAllWindows()
```

4. Save the file.

5. Open a terminal window.

6. Navigate to your working folder where the script is saved.

7. Type **sudo python view_video.py**.

A new window opens. It displays the video file that we recorded in the previous exercise. When the end of the file is reached, the video stops. Press Q to end the program and close the window.

Image Transformations

Now that you know more about how to get an image, let's take a look at some of the things that we can do with them. We will look at a few very basic operations. These operations were selected because they will help us reach our goal of tracking a ball. OpenCV is very powerful, and it has a lot more capabilities than I present here.

Flipping

Many times, the placement of the camera in a project is not ideal. Frequently, I've had to mount the camera upside down, or I've needed to flip the image for one reason or another.

Fortunately, OpenCV makes this very simple with the `flip()` method. The `flip()` method takes three parameters: the image to be flipped, the code indicating how to flip it, and the destination of the flipped image. The last parameter is only used if you want to assign the flipped image to another variable, but you can flip the image in place.

An image can be flipped horizontally, vertically, or both by providing the flipCode. The flipCode is positive, negative, or zero. Zero flips the image horizontally, a positive value flips it vertically, and a negative number flips it on both axes. More often than not, you will flip the image on both axes to effectively rotate it 180 degrees.

Let's use the image of the three balls that we used earlier to illustrate flipping a frame.

1. Open the IDLE IDE and create a new file.

2. Save the file as flip_image.py.

3. Enter the following code:

```python
import cv2

img = cv2.imread('color_balls_small.jpg')
h_img = cv2.flip(img, 0)
v_img = cv2.flip(img, 1)
b_img = cv2.flip(img, -1)

cv2.imshow('image', img)
cv2.imshow('horizontal', h_img)
cv2.imshow('vertical', v_img)
cv2.imshow('both', b_img)

cv2.waitKey(0)
```

4. Save the file.

5. Open a terminal window.

6. Navigate to the folder in which you saved the file.

7. Enter **python flip_image.py** and press Return.

Four windows open, each with a different version of the image file.
Press any key to exit.

Resizing

You can resize an image. This is useful for reducing the resources needed
to process an image. The larger the image, the more memory and CPU
resources needed. To resize an image, we use the `resize()` method. The
parameters are the image you are scaling, the desired dimensions as a
tuple, and the interpolation.

Interpolation is the mathematical method used for determining how to
handle the removal or addition of pixels. Remember, when working with
images, you are really working with a multidimensional array that contains
information for each point, or pixel, that makes up the image. When you
reduce an image, you are removing pixels. When you enlarge an image,
you are adding pixels. Interpolation is the method by which this occurs.

There are three interpolation options. INTER_AREA is best used
for reduction. INTER_CUBIC and INTER_LINEAR are both good for
enlarging an image, with INTER_LINEAR being the faster of the two. If an
interpolation is not provided, OpenCV uses INTER_LINEAR as the default
for both reducing and enlarging.

The image of the three balls is currently 800×533 pixels. Although it
isn't a large size, we will make it a little smaller. Let's make it half its current
size for both axes. To do this, we will use the INTER_AREA interpolation.

1. Open the IDLE IDE and create a new file.

2. Save the file as `resize_image.py`.

3. Enter the following code:

```
import cv2

img = cv2.imread('color_balls_small.jpg')
x,y = img.shape[:2]
resImg = cv2.resize(img, (y/2, x/2), interpolation =
cv2.INTER_AREA)

cv2.imshow('image', img)
cv2.imshow('resized', resImg)

cv2.waitKey(0)
```

4. Save the file.

5. Open a terminal window.

6. Navigate to the folder in which you saved the file.

7. Enter **python resize_image.py** and press Return.

Two windows should have opened. The first has the original image. The second displays the reduced image. Press any key to close the windows.

Working with Color

Color is obviously a very important part of working with images. As such, it is a very prominent part of OpenCV. There is a lot that can be done with color. We are going to focus on a few of the key elements needed to accomplish our end goal of identifying and chasing a ball with the robot.

Color Spaces

One of the key elements of working with color is *color space*, which describes how OpenCV expresses color. Within OpenCV, color is represented by a series of numbers. The color space determines the meaning of those numbers.

The default color space for OpenCV is BGR. This means every color is described by three integers between 0 and 255, which correspond to the three color channels—blue, green, and red, in that order. A color expressed as (255,0,0) has a maximum value in the blue channel, and both green and red are zero. This represents pure blue. Given this, (0,255,0) is green and (0,0,255) is red. The values (0,0,0) represent black, the absence of any color, and (255,255,255) is white.

If you've worked with graphics in the past, BGR is the opposite of what you're likely used to. Most digital graphics are described in terms of RGB—red, green, and blue. So, this may take a little getting used to.

There are many color spaces. The ones that we care about are BGR, RGB, HSV, and grayscale. We've already discussed the default color space, BGR, and the common RGB color space. HSV is hue, saturation, and value. Hue represents the color on a scale of 0 to 180. Saturation represents how far white the color is from 0 to 255. Value is a measure of how far from black the color is from 0 to 255. If both saturation and value are 0, the color is gray. A saturation and value of 255 is the brightest version of the hue.

Hue is a little trickier. It is on a scale of 0 to 180, where 0 and 180 are both red. This is where remembering the color wheel is important. If 0 and 180 meet at the top of the wheel in the middle of the red space, as you move clockwise around the wheel, hue = 30 is yellow, hue = 60 is green, hue = 90 is teal, hue = 120 is blue, hue = 150 is purple, and hue = 180 brings us back to red.

The one that you most frequently encounter is *grayscale*. Grayscale is exactly what it sounds like: the black-and-white version of an image. It is used by feature-detection algorithms to create masks. We use it when we filter for objects.

To convert an image to a different color space, you use the cvtColor method. It takes two parameters: the image and the color space constant. The color space constants are built into OpenCV. They are COLOR_BGR2RGB, COLOR_BGR2HSV, and COLOR_BGR2GRAY. Do you see the pattern there? If you wanted to convert from the RGB color space to the HSV color space, the constant would be COLOR_RGB2HSV.

Let's convert our image of the three colored balls to a grayscale image.

1. Open the IDLE IDE and create a new file.

2. Save the file as `gray_image.py`.

3. Enter the following code:

```
import cv2

img = cv2.imread('color_balls_small.jpg')
grayImg = cv2.cvtColor(img, cv2.COLOR_BGR2GRAY)

cv2.imshow('img', img)
cv2.imshow('gray', grayImg)

cv2.waitKey(0)
```

4. Save the file.

5. Open a terminal window.

6. Navigate to the folder in which you saved the file.

7. Enter **python gray_image.py** and press Return.

This opens two windows: one with the original color image and one with the grayscale version. Click any key to exit the program and close the windows.

Color Filters

Filtering for a color takes remarkably little code, but at the same time, it can be a little frustrating because you're generally not looking for a specific color but a color range. Colors are very rarely pure and of one value. This is why we want to be able to shift between color spaces. Sure, we could look for a red color in BGR. But to do that, we would need the specific range for each of the three values. And where that's going to hold true with all color spaces, it's generally easier to dial in the range you need in the HSV space.

The strategy used for filtering for a specific color is fairly straightforward, but there are a few steps involved and a couple things to keep in mind as you go.

First, we'll make a copy of the image in the HSV color space. Then we apply our filter range and make that its own image. For this, we use the `inRange()` method. It takes three parameters: the image we are applying the filter to, the lower range, and the upper range of values. The `inRange` method scans all the pixels in the provided image to determine if they are within the specified range. It returns true, or 1, if so; otherwise, it returns 0. What this leaves us with is a black-and-white image that we can use as a mask.

Next, we apply the mask using the `bitwise_and()` method. This method takes two images and returns the area where the pixels match. Since that's not quite what we are looking for, we need to do a little trickery. For our purpose, `bitwise_and` requires three parameters: image 1, image 2, and a mask. Since we want to return everything that is revealed by the mask, image 1 and image 2 both use our original image. Then we apply our mask by designating the mask parameter. Since we are leaving out a few optional parameters, we need to designate the mask parameter explicitly, like this: `mask = mask_image`. The result is an image that only shows the color we are filtering for.

The easiest way to demonstrate this is by walking through it. The code is actually quite simple once you know what's going on.

1. Open the IDLE IDE and create a new file.

2. Save the file as `blue_filter.py`.

3. Enter the following code:

```
import cv2

img = cv2.imread("color_balls_small.jpg")
imgHSV = cv2.cvtColor(img, cv2.COLOR_BGR2HSV)
```

```
lower_blue = np.array([80,120,120])
upper_blue = np.array([130,255,255])

blueMask = cv2.inRange(imgHSV,lower_blue,upper_blue)

res = cv2.bitwise_and(img, img, mask=blueMask)

cv2.imshow('img', img)
cv2.imshow('mask', blueMask)
cv2.imshow('blue', res)

cv2.waitKey(0)
```

4. Save the file.

5. Open a terminal window.

6. Navigate to the folder in which you saved the file.

7. Enter `python blue_filter.py` and press Return.

Three windows open with different versions of our image. The first is the regular image. The second is a black-and-white image that acts as our mask. The third is the final masked image. Only the pixels under the white area of the mask are displayed.

Let's take a moment to walk through the code to make it clear what we're doing and why.

We start like we do all of our scripts, with the importing of OpenCV and NumPy, and then loading the image.

```
import cv2
import numpy as np
img = cv2.imread("color_balls_small.jpg")
```

Next, we make a copy of the image and convert it to the HSV color space.

```
imgHSV = cv2.cvtColor(img, cv2.COLOR_BGR2HSV)
```

323

Once in the HSV color space, it is easier to filter for the blue ball. As I discussed, we know pure blue has a hue value of 120. Since it's unlikely the object that we are filtering for is pure blue, we need to give it a range of colors. In this case, we are looking for everything from 80, which is half way between green and blue, and 130. We also want to filter for colors that are not nearly white or nearly black, so we use the values 120 and 255 for the saturation and value ranges. To make sure that the filter range is in a format that OpenCV understands, we create them as NumPy arrays.

```
lower_blue = np.array([80,120,120])
upper_blue = np.array([130,255,255])
```

With the filter range specified, we can use them with the inRange() method to determine if the pixels in the HSV version of our image is in the blue range that we are looking for. This creates the mask image to exclude all non-blue pixels.

```
blueMask = cv2.inRange(imgHSV,lower_blue,upper_blue)
```

Next, we use bitwise_and() to apply our mask. Because we want to return all pixels from our image within our mask, we pass the original image as both image 1 and image 2. This compares the image against itself and returns the entire image, since every pixel in the image matches itself.

```
res = cv2.bitwise_and(img, img, mask=blueMask)
```

Finally, we display the original image, mask, and filtered image. Then we wait for a key to be pressed before we close the windows and exit the program.

```
cv2.imshow('img', img)
cv2.imshow('mask', blueMask)
cv2.imshow('blue', res)

cv2.waitKey(0)
```

As you can see, once you know how it works, filtering for a color is very easy. It gets a little more complicated when you are filtering for red. Red occurs at both the low and high ends of the hue spectrum, so you have to create two filters and combine the resulting masks. This can easily be done with OpenCV's add() method, and it looks something like this:

```
combinedMask = cv2.add(redMask1, redMask2)
```

In the end, you're left with an image with only the pixels that you are looking for. To the human eye, it is easily recognized as related groups. For the computer, it is not so. Natively, a computer does not recognize the difference between the black pixels and the blue. That's where blob detection comes into play.

Blobs and Blob Detection

A *blob* is a collection of similar pixels. They could be anything from a monotone circle to a jpeg image. To a computer, a pixel is a pixel, and it cannot distinguish between an image of a ball and an image of a plane. This is what makes computer vision so challenging. We have developed many different techniques to try to extrapolate information about an image; each has trade-offs in terms of speed and accuracy.

Most techniques use a process called *feature extraction*, which is a general term for a collection of algorithms that catalog outstanding features in an image, such as lines, edges, broad areas of color, and so forth. Once these features are extracted, they can be analyzed or compared with other features to make determinations about the image. This is how functions like face detection and motion detection work.

We are going to use a simpler method for tracking an object. Rather than extracting detailed features and analyzing them, we will use the color filtering techniques from the previous section to identify a large area of color. We will then use built-in functions to gather information about the group of pixels. This simpler technique is called *blob detection*.

Finding a Blob

OpenCV makes blob detection fairly easy, especially after we've done the heavy lifting of filtering out everything we don't want. Once the image has been filtered, we can use the mask for clean blob detection. The `SimpleBlobDetector` class from OpenCV identifies the location and the size of the blob.

The `SimpleBlobDetector` class is not quite as simple as you might think. There are a number of parameters built into it that need to be enabled or disabled. If enabled, you need to make sure that the values work for your application.

The method for setting the parameters is `SimpleBlobDetector_ Params()`. The method for creating the detector is `SimpleBlobDetector_ create()`. You pass the parameters to the create method to ensure everything is set properly.

Once the parameters are set and the detector is properly created, you use the `detect()` method to identify the keypoints. In the case of the simple blob detector, the keypoints represent the center and size of any detected blobs.

Finally, we use the `drawKeyPoints()` method to draw a circle around our blob. By default, this draws a small circle at the center of the blob. However, a flag can be passed that causes the size of the circle relative to the size of the blob.

Let's walk through an example. We'll use the filter code from the previous exercise and add blob detection. In this exercise, we filter for the blue ball in our image. Then we use the mask to find the center of the ball and draw a circle around it.

1. Open the IDLE IDE and create a new file.

2. Save the file as `simple_blob_detect.py`.

3. Enter the following code:

```
import cv2
import numpy as np

img = cv2.imread("color_balls_small.jpg")
imgHSV = cv2.cvtColor(img, cv2.COLOR_BGR2HSV)

# setup parameters
params = cv2.SimpleBlobDetector_Params()

params.filterByColor = False
params.filterByArea = False
params.filterByInertia = False
params.filterByConvexity = False
params.filterByCircularity = False

# create blob detector
det = cv2.SimpleBlobDetector_create(params)

lower_blue = np.array([80,120,120])
upper_blue = np.array([130,255,255])

blueMask = cv2.inRange(imgHSV,lower_blue,upper_blue)

res = cv2.bitwise_and(img, img, mask=blueMask)

# get keypoints
keypnts = det.detect(blueMask)

# draw keypoints
cv2.drawKeypoints(img, keypnts, img, (0,0,255),
        cv2.DRAW_MATCHES_FLAGS_DRAW_RICH_KEYPOINTS)

cv2.imshow('img', img)
cv2.imshow('mask', blueMask)
cv2.imshow('blue', res)
```

```
# print the coordinates and size of keypoints to terminal
for k in keypnts:
    print k.pt[0]
    print k.pt[1]
    print k.size

cv2.waitKey(0)
```

4. Save the file.

5. Open a terminal window.

6. Navigate to the folder in which you saved the file.

7. Enter **python simple_blob_detect.py** and press Return.

This opens the three versions of the image. However, the original image now has a red circle drawn around the blue ball. In the terminal window, we've printed the coordinates of the center of the ball as well as its size. The center of the ball is used later in this chapter when we start to track the ball.

The Parameters

The SimpleBlobDetector class takes several parameters to work properly. It is strongly suggested that all the filter options are explicitly enabled or disabled by setting the corresponding parameter to True or False. If a filter is enabled, you need to set the parameters for it as well. The default parameters are configured to extract dark circular blobs.

In the previous exercise, we simply disabled all the filters. Since we are working with a filtered image of a ball, and we only have the one blob in the image, we don't need to add other filters. Whereas you could technically use the parameters of the SimpleBlobDetector alone without masking out everything else, this can be a bit more challenging in dialing in all of the parameters to get the results we want. Also, the method we used allows you a little more insight as to what OpenCV is doing in the background.

It is important to understand how the SimpleBlobDetector works to have a better idea of how the filters are used. There are several parameters that can be used to fine-tune the results.

The first thing that happens is the image is converted into several binary images by applying thresholds. The `minThreshold` and `maxThreshold` determines the overall range, while the `thresholdStep` determines the distance between thresholds.

Each binary image is then processed for contours using `findContours()`. This allows the system to calculate the center of each blob. With the centers known, several blobs are combined into one group using the `minDistanceBetweenBlobs` parameter.

The center of the groups is returned as a keypoint, as is the overall diameter of the group. The parameters for each of the filters are calculated and the filters applied.

The Filters

The following lists the filters and their corresponding parameters.

filterByColor

This filters for the relative intensity of each binary image. It measures the intensity value at the center of the blobs and compares it to the parameter, `blobColor`. If they don't match, the blob does not qualify. The intensity is measured from 0 to 255; 0 is dark and 255 is light.

filterByArea

When the individual blobs are grouped, their overall area is calculated. This filter looks for blobs between `minArea` and `maxArea`.

filterByCircularity

Circularity is calculated by the formula

$$\frac{4 * \pi * Area}{perimeter * perimeter}$$

This returns a ratio between 0 and 1, which is compared to minCircularity and maxCircularity. If the value is between these parameters, the blob is included in the results.

filterByInertia

Inertia is an estimation of how elongated the blob is. It is a ratio between 0 and 1. If the value is between minInertiaRatio and maxInertiaRatio, the blob is returned in the keypoint results.

filterByConvexity

Convexity is a ratio with a value between 0 and 1. It measures the ratio between convex and concave curves in a blob. The parameters for convexity are minConvexity and maxConvexity.

Blob Tracking

We saw in the previous section that the x and y coordinates of the center of a blob are returned as part of the keypoints, which is used to track the blob. To track the blob, you need to use the live video stream from the robot's camera, and then define what tracking means for your project. The simplest form of tracking is simply moving the generated circle with the blob.

1.   Open the IDLE IDE and create a new file.

2.   Save the file as blob_tracker.py.

3. Enter the following code:

```
import cv2
import numpy as np

cap = cv2.VideoCapture(0)

# setup detector and parameters
params = cv2.SimpleBlobDetector_Params()

params.filterByColor = False
params.filterByArea = True
params.minArea = 20000
params.maxArea = 30000
params.filterByInertia = False
params.filterByConvexity = False
params.filterByCircularity = True
params.minCircularity = 0.5
params.maxCircularity = 1

det = cv2.SimpleBlobDetector_create(params)

# define blue
lower_blue = np.array([80,60,20])
upper_blue = np.array([130,255,255])

while True:
    ret, frame = cap.read()

    imgHSV = cv2.cvtColor(frame, cv2.COLOR_BGR2HSV)

    blueMask = cv2.inRange(imgHSV,lower_blue,upper_blue)
    blur= cv2.blur(blueMask, (10,10))

    res = cv2.bitwise_and(frame, frame, mask=blueMask)
```

```
            # get and draw keypoint
            keypnts = det.detect(blur)

            cv2.drawKeypoints(frame, keypnts, frame, (0,0,255),
                            cv2.DRAW_MATCHES_FLAGS_DRAW_RICH_
                            KEYPOINTS)

            cv2.imshow('frame', frame)
            cv2.imshow('mask', blur)

            for k in keypnts:
                print k.size

            if cv2.waitKey(1) & 0xff == ord('q'):
                break

    cap.release()
    cv2.destroyAllWindows()
```

4. Save the file.

5. Open a terminal window.

6. Navigate to the folder in which you saved the file.

7. Enter **sudo python blob_tracker.py** and press Return.

Two windows open: one showing the mask used for filtering the color and one with the video stream. A circle should be drawn around the blob.

I enabled `filterByArea` and `filterByCircularity` to make sure that I am only getting the ball. You will likely need to make adjustments to the detector's parameters to fine-tune your filter.

Ball-Chasing Bot

You now know how to track a blob with the webcam mounted on the robot. In Chapter 8, you learned about an algorithm to follow a line called a PID controller. What happens when we combine the PID controller with our ball-tracking program?

Next, let's program the little robot to chase that blue ball that it's been tracking. To do this, you will use what you just learned about blob tracking and what you learned in Chapter 8.

The PID controller is expecting input in the form of deviation from the desired result. So, we need to start by defining the desired result. In this case, the goal is simply to keep the ball in the middle of the frame. So our error values will be the variance from the center, which also means that we need to define the center of the frame. Once we have the center defined, the deviation is a matter of subtracting the x location of the ball from the x location of the center. We will also subtract the y location of the ball from the y location of the center.

Now we can use two PID controllers to keep the ball centered in the frame. The first controller steers the robot. As the ball moves on the x axis, the deviation is either negative or positive. If it's positive, steer to the left. If it's negative, steer to the right. In the same manner, we can use the y axis to control the velocity of the robot. A positive y variance drives the robot forward, whereas a negative variance drives it backward.

1. Open the IDLE IDE and create a new file.

2. Save the file as ball_chaser.py.

3. Enter the following code:

```
import cv2
import numpy as np
import time
```

```
from Adafruit_MotorHAT import Adafruit_MotorHAT as amhat
from Adafruit_MotorHAT import Adafruit_DCMotor as adamo

# create motor objects
motHAT = amhat(addr=0x60)
mot1 = motHAT.getMotor(1)
mot2 = motHAT.getMotor(2)
mot3 = motHAT.getMotor(3)
mot4 = motHAT.getMotor(4)

motors = [mot1, mot2, mot3, mot4]

# motor multipliers
motorMultiplier = [1.0, 1.0, 1.0, 1.0, 1.0]

# motor speeds
motorSpeed = [0,0,0,0]

# speeds
speedDef = 100
leftSpeed = speedDef
rightSpeed = speedDef
diff= 0
maxDiff = 50
turnTime = 0.5

# create camera object
cap = cv2.VideoCapture(0)
time.sleep(1)

# PID
kp = 1.0
ki = 1.0
kd = 1.0
ballX = 0.0
ballY = 0.0
```

```python
x = {'axis':'X',
     'lastTime':int(round(time.time()*1000)),
     'lastError':0.0,
     'error':0.0,
     'duration':0.0,
     'sumError':0.0,
     'dError':0.0,
     'PID':0.0}
y = {'axis':'Y',
     'lastTime':int(round(time.time()*1000)),
     'lastError':0.0,
     'error':0.0,
     'duration':0.0,
     'sumError':0.0,
     'dError':0.0,
     'PID':0.0}

# setup detector
params = cv2.SimpleBlobDetector_Params()

# define detector parameters
params.filterByColor = False
params.filterByArea = True
params.minArea = 15000
params.maxArea = 40000
params.filterByInertia = False
params.filterByConvexity = False
params.filterByCircularity = True
params.minCircularity = 0.5
params.maxCircularity = 1

# create blob detector object
det = cv2.SimpleBlobDetector_create(params)
```

```python
# define blue
lower_blue = np.array([80,60,20])
upper_blue = np.array([130,255,255])

def driveMotors(leftChnl = speedDef, rightChnl = speedDef,
                duration = defTime):
    # determine the speed of each motor by multiplying
    # the channel by the motors multiplier
    motorSpeed[0] = leftChnl * motorMultiplier[0]
    motorSpeed[1] = leftChnl * motorMultiplier[1]
    motorSpeed[2] = rightChnl * motorMultiplier[2]
    motorSpeed[3] = rightChnl * motorMultiplier[3]

    # set each motor speed. Since the speed can be a
    # negative number, we take the absolute value
    for x in range(4):
        motors[x].setSpeed(abs(int(motorSpeed[x])))

    # run the motors. if the channel is negative, run
    # reverse. else run forward
    if(leftChnl < 0):
        motors[0].run(amhat.BACKWARD)
        motors[1].run(amhat.BACKWARD)
    else:
        motors[0].run(amhat.FORWARD)
        motors[1].run(amhat.FORWARD)

    if (rightChnl > 0):
        motors[2].run(amhat.BACKWARD)
        motors[3].run(amhat.BACKWARD)
    else:
        motors[2].run(amhat.FORWARD)
        motors[3].run(amhat.FORWARD)
```

```python
def PID(axis):
    lastTime = axis['lastTime']
    lastError = axis['lastError']

    # get the current time
    now = int(round(time.time()*1000))
    duration = now-lastTime

    # calculate the error
    axis['sumError'] += axis['error'] * duration
    axis['dError'] = (axis['error'] - lastError)/duration

    # prevent runaway values
    if axis['sumError'] > 1:axis['sumError'] = 1
    if axis['sumError'] < -1: axis['sumError'] = -1

    # calculate PID
    axis['PID'] = kp * axis['error'] + ki *
    axis['sumError'] + kd * axis['dError']

    # update variables
    axis['lastError'] = axis['error']
    axis['lastTime'] = now

    # return the output value
    return axis

def killMotors():
    mot1.run(amhat.RELEASE)
    mot2.run(amhat.RELEASE)
    mot3.run(amhat.RELEASE)
    mot4.run(amhat.RELEASE)
```

```python
# main program
try:
    while True:
        # capture video frame
        ret, frame = cap.read()

        # calculate center of frame
        height, width, chan = np.shape(frame)
        xMid = width/2 * 1.0
        yMid = height/2 * 1.0

        # filter image for blue ball
        imgHSV = cv2.cvtColor(frame, cv2.COLOR_BGR2HSV)

        blueMask = cv2.inRange(imgHSV, lower_blue,
        upper_blue)
        blur = cv2.blur(blueMask, (10,10))

        res = cv2.bitwise_and(frame,frame,mask=blur)

        # get keypoints
        keypoints = det.detect(blur)
        try:
            ballX = int(keypoints[0].pt[0])
            ballY = int(keypoints[0].pt[1])
        except:
            pass

        # draw keypoints
        cv2.drawKeypoints(frame, keypoints, frame,
        (0,0,255),
                          cv2.DRAW_MATCHES_FLAGS_DRAW_
                          RICH_KEYPOINTS)
```

```
# calculate error and get PID ratio
xVariance = (ballX - xMid) / xMid
yVariance = (yMid - ballY) / yMid

x['error'] = xVariance/xMid
y['error'] = yVariance/yMid

x = PID(x)
y = PID(y)

# calculate left and right speeds
leftSpeed = (speedDef * y['PID']) + (maxDiff *
x['PID'])
rightSpeed = (speedDef * y['PID']) - (maxDiff *
x['PID'])

# another safety check for runaway values
if leftSpeed > (speedDef + maxDiff): leftSpeed
= (speedDef + maxDiff)
if leftSpeed < -(speedDef + maxDiff): leftSpeed
= -(speedDef + maxDiff)
if rightSpeed > (speedDef + maxDiff):
rightSpeed = (speedDef + maxDiff)
if rightSpeed < -(speedDef + maxDiff):
rightSpeed = -(speedDef + maxDiff)

# drive motors
driveMotors(leftSpeed, rightSpeed, driveTime)

# show frame
##      cv2.imshow('frame', frame)
##      cv2.waitKey(1)
```

```
except KeyboardInterrupt:
    killMotors()
    cap.release()
    cv2.destroyAllWindows()
```

4. Save the file.

5. Open a terminal window.

6. Navigate to the folder in which you saved the file.

7. Enter **sudo python ball_chaser.py** and press Return.

After a couple seconds, your robot should start moving forward. If there is a blue ball within the frame, it should turn toward it. The robot is trying to keep the ball in the center of the frame.

A few things in this code are a little different from the way we've done things in the past. Most notably, we put the values for the x and y axes into dictionaries. We did this to keep the values together when we passed them to the PID controller, which is another change that was made. The PID function was updated to accept a single parameter. However, the parameter it is expecting is a dictionary. It is assigned to the axis variable in the function. All the variable references are then updated to use the dictionary. The results are updated within the axis dictionary, and are then assigned to the appropriate dictionary in the main program.

I also made sure to remove any delays that would affect the main loop or the cameras refresh rate. Because this entire program is running in a single process, it is not as fast as it would be if we were to break the processes into different threads. As such, the robot may miss the ball and wander off.

Summary

In this chapter, we started to harness some of the exciting capabilities that the Raspberry Pi offers. Computer vision allows us to perform much more complex tasks than we can with microcontrollers alone.

To prepare for working with vision, we installed a basic webcam on the robot. This took special consideration since these webcams are not designed to be mounted. Of course, your solution is likely different than mine, so you were able to exercise some creativity in mounting the camera. After that, we were ready to install OpenCV.

OpenCV is an open source community-developed computer vision platform that makes many vision functions very simple. Installing the software on the Raspberry Pi takes quite a while, mostly because we have to compile it from source code, and despite its impressive capabilities, the Raspberry Pi doesn't have the processing power of a laptop or a PC, so it takes a while to compile the code. But once compiled and installed, we are able to do some fun things.

We worked through some exercises using a still image. This allowed us to learn some of the fundamentals of OpenCV without the overhead of processing video. Once we learned some of the basics, we learned to pull live video from the camera and apply the lessons we learned using still images. Using the color filtering and blob tracking techniques we picked up in this chapter, we gave our robot the capability to see and follow a ball.

CHAPTER 10

Conclusion

You've come a long way since Chapter 1. If you were new to robotics and programming, then this was probably a challenging book. It was intended to be, so congratulations on making it through. Hopefully, you followed along and built your own robot in the process.

To recap, in Chapter 1, I introduced some of the basic concepts of robots and discussed the purpose of the book. In Chapter 2, we began working with the Raspberry Pi by installing the Raspbian operating system and configuring it for remote access. Chapter 3 introduced you to the Python programming language. In Chapter 4, we started working with sensors using Raspberry Pi's GPIO header. In the process, we learned a bit about digital processing and discussed some of the limitations.

The solution to the Pi's limitations was introduced in Chapter 5 when I presented you with the Arduino. We learned how to program the Arduino and how to pass data back and forth between it and the Pi. In Chapter 6, we assembled the Motor HAT and learned how to drive motors with it and with a generic motor controller. In Chapter 7, we finally assembled the robot. In Chapter 8, we attached IR sensors and programmed the robot to follow a line. And in Chapter 9, we unleashed the power of the Raspberry Pi to use computer vision to filter for a color and track a ball.

© Jeff Cicolani 2018
J. Cicolani, *Beginning Robotics with Raspberry Pi and Arduino*,
https://doi.org/10.1007/978-1-4842-3462-4_10

Types of Robotics

As I discussed in Chapter 1, *robotics* can mean a lot of different things. It really depends on how you want to define it. To help obfuscate the definition even further, many of the technologies used in robotics are easily transferable to the Internet of Things (IoT). The hardware, software, sensors, communication channels, and so forth, are the same in your automated home as in your robot. The programming is similar and the results usually affect the physical world. So, in essence, IoT turns your home, office, or factory into a robot.

Due to this broad definition, your interest in robotics may differ greatly than mine. For instance, are you interested in little table bots or in larger robots? Are you primarily interested in terrestrial robots that drive along the ground, or do you want your automated apparatus to take flight? Or, maybe you're interested in exploring the depths of the sea with a robotic submersible. Do you want to experiment with autonomous cars or is home automation and IoT your thing?

Knowing the fields that you will likely pursue determines the tools that you use. If you're building little tabletop robots, you likely won't need a welder. The field also determines some of the design tools that you will use. For instance, most small robots like the one we built in this book can be designed on the fly or with pen and paper. However, if you're building something more complex, like a quadruped, you may need CAD software.

Tools

Tools come in two flavors in robotics: hardware and software. I didn't go into the physical hardware tools that you will likely use because the types of tools you'll use depend on the type of robotics that interest you. I will get to hardware in a moment.

First, I want to talk a little bit about software. Software is one area that is shared across all areas of robotics. Like most things in robotics, your choice of tools is entirely up to you. Use what you're comfortable with and gets the job done.

Software

The topics covered in this book were far from comprehensive. There is a lot more to learn about Linux, Python, Arduino, and especially OpenCV. The intent was to introduce you to some of the concepts of robotics, and to get you familiar and comfortable with some of the tools.

Choosing an IDE

The IDE, or *integrated development environment,* that you use is up to you. This is one of the areas shared across all the various fields. There are many to choose from. The software tools we used are native to the Raspberry Pi and the Arduino. And by "native" I mean that these are tools built into the OS or are the recommended tools for the hardware.

In all actuality, outside of writing this book, I do not use the IDLE IDE any longer. My general workflow starts on my Windows machine. When the code is working the way I like, I transfer it over to the Raspberry Pi for the finishing touches.

My preferred tool for programming Python is PyCharm (`www.jetbrains.com/pycharm`). The Community Edition offers all the features I need for almost all of my projects. It is a professional-level IDE that makes working with Python much easier (see Figure 10-1). It is available for both Windows and Linux. So, when I transfer the files to the Pi, I can use the same tools to update the code, as needed.

Figure 10-1. *PyCharm IDE*

Spyder is another excellent IDE for working with Python. It is included with the Anaconda distribution of Python, which makes installation a little easier. It offers many tools aimed at the scientific and academic communities. Anaconda is very popular with many of the data scientists I work with.

If you are interested in checking out Anaconda, you can find it at www.anaconda.com. Or, if you want to try the Spyder IDE, you can download it at https://pythonhosted.org/spyder/.

Also, Microsoft's Visual Studio is a very powerful and increasingly accessible product. Again, their Community Edition is available for download from their website (www.visualstudio.com). Once upon a time, Visual Studio was for professional developers only. Even when Microsoft started releasing the free Community Edition, it was difficult for beginners and hobbyists to use. However, the last few releases are more user-friendly.

One of the nice things about Visual Studio is that it can be used for most of your development needs.

It does have its drawbacks, though. For instance, it is only available for Windows. It still has a bit of a learning curve, too, but there are plenty of resources available to help. As a Windows-based IDE, it compiles for Windows. Fortunately, Python is cross-platform. So once you've written your code, you can transfer the Python files to the Raspberry Pi, make any adjustments you need for the serial port and so forth, and then run it from there.

I still use the Arduino IDE for most of my Arduino work. This is simply because I have not found a better independent environment on which to work. Visual Studio has an extension that allows you to develop Arduino code and cross compile to the Arduino; although it does the compilation through the Arduino IDE. So, if you're looking for a single environment to develop your robotics projects, Visual Studio may be a good choice.

Design Software

Many of you may not use design software with any frequency. As with everything else, the software used to design the various parts of your robot will vary depending on your project. It will also vary depending on your budget and the tools that you use to build your robot. Some projects, such as kits or someone else's design, won't require design software at all. Many projects and building styles get away with simple pencil and paper. If you are using modular parts, you may be able to get away with lists or simple sketches. For anything custom, however, you will probably need a way to design the system.

2D Drawing

The simplest and easiest to use software is for 2D—or flat—designs. These tools are good for designing projects that can be built using sheet materials such as MDF, cardboard, plywood, or acrylic sheets. Don't underestimate what you can do with flat material. My Nomad project is designed and built using 1/4-inch plywood.

Keep in mind that these tools are designed for artists and illustrators, not for precision CAD work. So some of the features you might expect are simply not there. For instance, precise measurements are difficult. Using grids and rulers help considerably, but if you need a precise angle or length, these tools may not be the best for the job.

One of the most popular 2D design tools is an open source project called Inkscape (`https://inkscape.org/en/`). Inkscape is remarkably easy to use, and it has a very large community of users. It is free to download and use, and it is rich with features. There are also many community-developed plugins. One of my favorites is the tabbed box maker. Since I have access to a laser cutter, I use the tabbed box maker to design simple boxes that I can cut and snap together. Figure 10-2 shows the Inkscape interface.

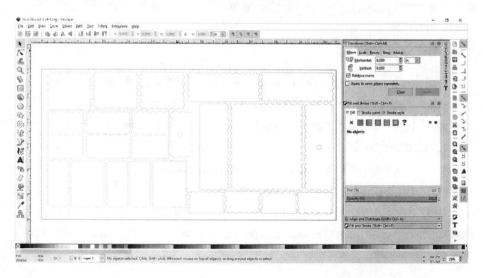

Figure 10-2. *Inkscape*

There are also commercial programs available. Adobe Illustrator (`www.adobe.com/products/illustrator.html`) and Corel Draw (`www.coreldraw.com/en/pages/ppc/coreldraw/`) are the two leaders in this area.

Circuit Board Design

At some point, you may find yourself needing to design your own circuit boards or shield. This isn't as complex or difficult as you may think. As you work more and more with robotics, you will find recommendations for specific chips or circuits. Often, simply searching online provides links to example circuits. Re-creating these circuits in a tool designed for it allows you to order the board.

There are many programs designed for circuit boards. In fact, almost every circuit board manufacturer has one available.

One of the most popular in the hobby community is Fritzing (http://fritzing.org/home/). It was developed at the University of Applied Science Potsdam in Germany. Its popularity has led it to be spun off into its own organization: the Friends-of-Fritzing Foundation. I used Fritzing software to create the circuit diagrams in this book (see Figure 10-3).

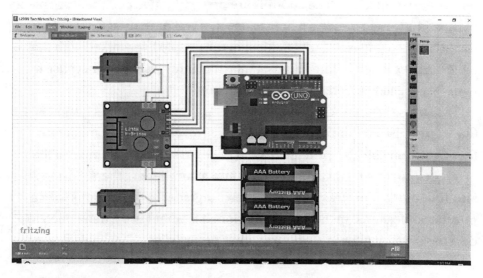

Figure 10-3. *Fritzing*

There are also commercial products available; many of them have free to use community additions. The leading industry standard is Eagle, which is now owned by Autodesk (`www.autodesk.com/products/eagle/overview`). Most other programs import and/or export final designs in the popular Eagle format.

3D Design

If you have a custom chassis and parts, or if you like 3D printing, you need 3D CAD software. Again, there are many available. But I have not found a free or open source package that matches the commercial solutions. That being said, many of the commercial solutions have student versions offered for free or at a reduced price.

SketchUp (`www.sketchup.com`) offers a free version of software designed for makers. If you have never used a CAD program before, it may be the easiest to learn. The controls are pretty intuitive and there are plenty of tutorials to help you learn how to use it. If you have used CAD before, then this probably isn't for you. Most of the people I've worked with that have CAD experience find this tool less than intuitive. That's because it wasn't designed as a standard CAD program.

For those of you more familiar with CAD, Autodesk offers Fusion 360 (`www.autodesk.com/products/fusion-360/overview`) for a moderate fee. The company also provides free licenses to students for most of their products, such as Fusin 360, Inventor, and a number of others. Fusion 360 and Inventor are professional, commercial-grade CAD programs with a number of features, including simulation. It is what I use when I need to design something for my robots or other projects (see Figure 10-4).

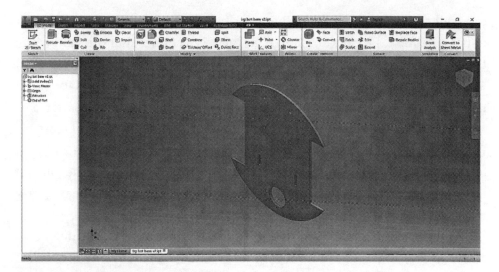

Figure 10-4. *Autodesk Inventor*

Hardware

In addition to the software tools that I described, you need some actual tools. Your choice of tools is probably most dependent on the type of robotics that interests you, but there are some basics that every toolbox should have.

Basic Tools

In this section, I cover the tools that you will likely need, regardless of the form your robot or project takes, and the tools that are in my base kit.

First, a good set of pliers is a must. You need different sizes and types. The ones I use the most are the set of jeweler's pliers. I also frequently use slip-joint pliers. Make sure that the set includes a pair of diagonal cutters.

Next in your kit, you want to have a good set of fine screwdrivers. Many of the screws you use are small and fit in tight places. Make sure that there is a variety of hex heads in your set. Frequently, I find that the hex screw I am trying to insert or remove is between two sizes in my set. The star heads usually fit these. Be careful, though, as there is a chance that you can strip the teeth off them.

From here, there are a lot of miscellaneous tools that are good to have: a utility knife, an array of files, a crimping tool, a flush wire cutter, a multimeter, calipers, and so forth. You'll gather a good selection of tools. I strongly suggest that you buy the tools that you need, rather than try to make do with what you have on hand. Using the right tool for the job always bears better results. And, if you take the time to acquire the proper tool, you'll have it the next time you need it.

You also need a soldering station. It doesn't have to be elaborate. A good soldering iron, a place for your flux and tip cleaner, and a set of helping hands is the extent of what you need.

Make sure that you have a good place to keep the tools, and try to always put them back. This saves you countless hours from searching through the inevitable clutter in your workspace. I have several sets of tools. One set lives on my workbench. I bought a compact pegboard system on which to hang most of my tools. What doesn't fit on the pegboard goes into specific drawers on the bench.

Another set is in a toolbox that I leave with Nomad. Since Nomad is frequently taken to shows, and soon competitions, I want to make sure that I always have what I need on-hand. More often than not, I end up helping the other presenters at the shows since they are frequently ill prepared.

My third set of tools is a floating set. I keep them in a toolbox that is easily ported from room to room or to the car when I venture out without Nomad. I'm active in the local hobby robotics scene in Austin, and it's good to be prepared when someone needs a hand or a tool.

I try to make sure to always put my tools back where they belong when I'm done using them. This assures that the next time I reach for a tool, it's there. Admittedly, I'm not as consistent as I'd like to be, but it is a really good habit to get into.

Specialty Tools

Having some of the larger, specialty tools always makes my larger builds easier. A band saw and a drill press are invaluable. Unless you are planning to build some very large robots, the benchtop version of both of these tools will usually suffice. A benchtop belt/disk sander combination help clean up your edges or shape your parts.

In addition to all of these tools, I make use of more specialized tools. For the most part, I don't have these tools at home. But 3D printers are fairly easy to get these days; if possible, having one or two in your workshop is a good idea. I also make use of a 120W laser cutter, CNC routers, and CNC mills. They are not tools that I have in my shop, however.

Makerspaces

I don't have laser cutters and CNC mills in my home shop, as I imagine most of you don't either. These tools are bulky and expensive. But, I am a member of the local makerspace in Austin: the ATX Hackerspace (http://atxhs.org). The Hackerspace is a co-op workshop where we have been able to pull together our resources to purchase some of the larger machines. What the Hackerspace doesn't own is frequently hosted by a member for other members to use.

What makes the space particularly valuable is the community. Makerspaces are full of people who like to create things. These people come from every walk of life and have individual skills. This is a very valuable resource when you are trying to do something you've never done before, or you want to learn a new skill, or you want a different perspective on a problem, or you are just plain stuck.

These days, almost every community has one or more makerspaces. The resources available vary from space to space. Some operate in commercial parks, some at schools, and some out of someone's garage. The one thing that remains constant is the community. If you haven't already, find your local makerspace and join it. You won't regret it.

Summary

You now have all the basics that you need to get started in hobby robotics. There is obviously a lot more to learn in many topics. But, the Raspberry Pi and the Arduino will take you a long way. Remember, you don't need to learn everything in a vacuum. There is a huge community out there, and it is growing every day. Reach out to your local makerspace to find like-minded builders. Don't be afraid to ask questions. Don't be afraid to look at other people's projects for inspiration. Take advantage of sample code whenever possible. Eventually, you will write your own code, but until then, learn from those that have already done it.

The field of robotics is exciting. The fact that we can enter into it, experiment, and learn is phenomenal. Take advantage of this time. Most importantly, have fun.

Good luck and happy building.

Index

A

R

Get the eBook for only $5!

Why limit yourself?

With most of our titles available in both PDF and ePUB format, you can access your content wherever and however you wish—on your PC, phone, tablet, or reader.

Since you've purchased this print book, we are happy to offer you the eBook for just $5.

To learn more, go to http://www.apress.com/companion or contact support@apress.com.

Apress®

CPSIA information can be obtained
at www.ICGtesting.com
Printed in the USA
LVOW10s2035270418
575135LV00002B/6/P